Writers of the Waveney Valley

I have used the term Waveney Valley loosely, this book is intended as a record of writers who live and have lived in the area roughly from Diss to Lowestoft and Gt. Yarmouth, and of a few writers who have written of their journey through the area.

Some have written novels, others of their expeditions, many reflect the time they are living in, starting with Skelton who put into verse his opposition to the power of the church hierarchy before the reformation.

In the C18th outstanding women like Anne Barbauld wrote specifically for children and Elizabeth Bonhote wrote for the female market, both ahead of their time. The poet Crabbe, expresses his opposition to the work-house and his concern for the poor. Thomas Manning kept a journal of his visit to China as early as 1806 and Sir Samuel Baker recorded his explorations of the Nile in great detail.

The sense of injustice at how the C19th poor are treated is reflected by Richard Cobbold, rector of Wortham for 52 years. Diaries tell us of J Barber Scott's meeting with Napoleon ,and George Borrow, living at Oulton, near Lowestoft, tells the reader of Spain and the gypsy life with tales of his travels.

Sir Rider Haggard incorporated his early working life experiences in South Africa into his adventure novels, which had a huge following, and he used his later travels along with his own farming experience to report to the government on the state of farming in Denmark and the UK.

There are military men who have recorded their memoirs and farmer/writers, such as Adrian Bell who have told us of the changes in agriculture during the first half of the C20th based on their own working life.

During the latter half of the C20th people such as Roger Deakin began to raise awareness of mankind's effect on planet Earth and other writers such as Richard Mabey have continued this work. The novelist Louis de Bernieres weaves the early 1900s Greek/Turkey situation into his book 'Birds without Wings' and a film was made of his 'Captain Correlli's Mandolin', set in Greece. Terence Blacker shares his unique view of life through his novels and national newspaper column.

Adrian Bloom and Philip Wayre have produced works relating to their work or business, others of their absorbing interests, for example Elaine Murphy, Christopher Reeve and Ian McLachlan.

I have had the pleasure of meeting some of the latter writers, living along or near the Waveney Valley, who like all the people in this book want to record and share with us their knowledge, experiences and opinions.

The river Waveney was used for transport by people as well as for goods and there were several religious establishments along the river, such as the St Olave's Augustinian Priory founded in 1239 at Herringfleet, near where the ferry crossed the Waveney, a convent at Bungay, a priory at Mendham. With poor roads, and no stage-coaches until at least 1620, it was easier to travel by boat, especially when moving from church to church or religious house.

There were water-mills along the river, some mentioned in the Domesday Book, at Syleham, Needham, Weybread, Mendham and Limbourne Mill at Wortwell. Most milled corn for flour or animal feed. Hemp was grown along the valley bottom and the area was known for its dairy farming.

The 95km river rises between Redgrave and Lopham near Diss, meandering easterly until it flows into Breydon Water, where it joins the river Yare and reaches the sea at nearby Gt Yarmouth. From there it is tidal as far inland as Beccles.

A 1670 Act of Parliament extended navigation of the river up to the town of Bungay. The wherries used on the Waveney for commercial trade had a maximum size of 70' x 16', with a counter-balanced mast so that they could pass under bridges easily.

The foot-bridge at Homersfield, with its 50' span, was built in 1869 and was one of the first to be constructed from concrete and iron. The Lowestoft to Norwich railway line crossed the river at Somerleyton on a swing bridge, which became double tracked in 1905.

Mendham Priory

was founded in 1140 by William, son of Roger de Huntingfield, and was part of the Cluniac order; this French order of monks had first set up a priory in Lewes in the late C11th, and some 30 years later Thetford Priory was being built. John de Lindsey was the first Prior of Mendham; there were generally eight monks living there. The priory was dissolved in 1537,but some of the building materials can still be found in other Mendham buildings.

Some of the monks would have copied manuscripts; there is evidence that much earlier, Romans had lived in the Waveney Valley, and they had links to a larger settlement at Caister St Edmunds near Norwich.

Thomas Bungay about 1214-1294

Born in Bungay and educated at Oxford and Paris he became a Franciscan friar in Norwich. Living at Oxford and Cambridge as a Franciscan master, he wrote on theological matters.

1400-1700

With the river and poor roads as the only means of travel and communication, it would have taken the writers from this period days to journey as far as they did, for their education, maintaining contact with other communities, and locating from one residence to another part of the country.

Skelton travelled from Diss to Oxford, Cambridge and London before returning to Diss and we have a record of him going to Norwich. Suckling, who died in France, owned land and property in other counties as well as having a London home. Broome came over 200 miles away from Crewe to live and work in Eye and Pulham, but at the end of his life died in Bath.

Skelton lived during an entirely Catholic period and would have known of land owning priories, and of their demands on their neighbourhoods. He would have been aware of the introduction of the printing press in 1476, but it was about 10 years after his death that a printed bible would have been seen in parish churches.

Broome, born at least 200 years after Skelton, would not have experienced the upheaval of the reformation or the civil war, and the political see-saw of Catholic James 11 following after his protestant father Charles 11. Living at the time of Jonathan Swift (1667-1745), and Samuel Johnson (1709-1784), Broome may have lived studiously in south Norfolk, but his connections with the local Cornwallis family and Alexander Pope (1688-1744) would have assured his knowledge of life in London, the rise in world-wide trade and exploration and the establishment of institutions such as the Bank of England in 1694.

Suckling would have had estate managers to control his different lands and to ensure an income for his lifestyle. The name of Suckling has been associated with the village of Barsham near Beccles for hundreds of years, and is where Adrian Bell (1901-1980) lies buried.

These three writers received formal education and spent time at university (Oxford, established by 1167, and Cambridge established by 1209; other than medical schools the next university to be established was Durham in 1832), such a contrast to the general population with no education other than 'dame schools' or early grammar schools. Poor children did not attend school as their labour was invaluable to the family.

With the UK population estimated to be under 5 million between 1600 and 1700, much of the land was arable or pasture, with many people working on the land, particularly in East Anglia. In the Waveney valley hemp and flax were grown, the Diss Friday market being famous for its linen cloth. The first record of Diss market is in 1275, the same year as Acle. There is still a Friday market in Diss today.

Daniel Defoe (1660-1731) mentions other market towns, Beccles, Bungay and Harleston when he travelled along the Waveney Valley. These small self-sufficient communities he termed 'good market towns' yet those living there would have known the effect of the plague from time to time, and childhood deaths from influenza and infection. In the late C15th and early C16th if a person reached the age of 30 there was a good chance that they would live until they were nearly 60.

John **Skelton**, Diss 1460?-1529

Thought to have been born in Diss, after an education partly in Cambridge, partly in Oxford, Skelton received an MA degree in 1484. He was admitted to Holy Orders in 1498 and became Rector of Diss in 1504, where he was the Catholic parish priest for 25 years in pre-Reformation times. He was created 'poet-laureate' by Cambridge & Oxford universities; before he became tutor to Prince Henry, son of Henry V11, he was resident clerk and teacher to the Howard family (Duke of Norfolk) in Kenninghall. In 1512-13 he became court poet and rhetorician to Henry V111. Erasmus called him 'the one light and ornament of the British Isles'.

Writing his poetry and manuscripts with a quill pen and probably using iron gall ink, his works were printed from as early as 1523.

Road sign off Victoria Road in Diss

1399-1461 Henry 1V, V and V1,   1400, population of Norwich nearly 4,000.

1461-1483 Edward 1V,   Caxton printing press introduced to England 1476

1483 Edward V,   1483-1485 Richard 111,

1485-1509 Henry V11,   1509-1547 Henry V111.

56 people died in the Diss plague of 1579

His poems include 'The Bowge of Court', 'Garlande of Laurell', 'Phylyp Sparrowe', 'Colyn Cloute', 'The Tunning of Eleanor Rumming', and satires such as 'Why cam ye nat to courte' and 'Speke Parrot'. Written in 1521 the latter is regarded as Skelton's masterpiece - it is a complex attempt to show the position of the poet in a corrupt world of absolute power.

With his attacks on Cardinal Wolsey he made many enemies and was suspended by the Bishop of the diocese for 'disobedience to the rule of clerical celibacy'. Wolsey finally compelled him to seek the sanctuary of Abbott John Islip at Westminster, where he died in 1529 and was buried in the chancel of St Margaret's church (in the grounds of Westminster Abbey).

A biography of Norfolk Celebrities dated 1876, held at NRO (MC257/86-91) includes Skelton and reads " John Skelton, the satirical poet flourished in the early part of the reign of King Henry VIII, and was rector of Diss in this county. Amongst English poets of note he comes near to Chaucer and is celebrated for his satirical lampoons. Most of Skelton's satires are levelled at the clergy of his time, and so severe were some of them that they raised up against him many bitter enemies, in so much that he found it necessary at last to take flight from his rectory…...

In his sermons Skelton severely satirised the Mendicant order and others of his own calling and thus rendered himself extremely unpopular amongst the priesthood, he was severely admonished and censored and some think, suspended by his diocesan, Nykke, who is noted in history as 'the arbitrary Bishop of Norwich' (Richard Nykke 1447-1535 was the last Roman Catholic Bishop of Norwich). It is believed he was punished by this prelate 'for being guilty of certain crimes as most poets are', the crime in question being that Skelton had had the weakness to take to himself a wife.

As may readily be supposed these persecutions and arbitrary punishments did not tend to soften the rather acrimonious character of John Skelton, nor did they tend to put an end to his keen satire. His convictions were strong and earnest and fear is generally a stranger to such natures as Skelton's. Persecution but embitters such dispositions as his...when Skelton was deprived of making himself heard from the pulpit, he commenced writing more scathing lampoons in verse. With the courage of his class our poet sometimes shot at very high fame, and Cardinal Wolsey being amongst his real or supposed enemies Skelton had the courageous audacity to accuse the great Cardinal Minister when at the height of his power and fame and was consequently pursued by the spies and officers of that Statesman. Skelton was taken to Westminster Abbey and obtained the protection of Bishop Islip who sheltered him."

Diss in 1460, St. Mary's church has C15th porches and windows. The church is thought to stand on the site of a late Saxon church. The tower and nave arcades date from 1290, much of the church is dated from the C14th .Two chancel chapels were built in the C15th by the two trade guilds of the town. Diss was made prosperous during the mediaeval period through the cloth and wool trade. Skelton may have seen St. Nicholas chapel being built during the C15th, this was dissolved and destroyed during the Reformation. Fair Green, Diss, has been the site of a market and fair for 800 years.

An earlier biography (NRO MS20438) describes Skelton in the same way, "many years Rector of Dysse in Norfolk, he disgraced the Church by his conduct and abused it in his words; especially violent were his invectives against Wolsey. He wrote 'Merrie Tales', not all very decent….Skelton did keep a market at Dysse upon which he was complained of to the Bishop of Norwich. Being sent for, he took with him two capons: on being upbraided for his conduct he said "Is this what you want with me? God be with you" and he went his way. But after all, he was invited to dine at the Palace, and the capons were accepted, which he gave with this proviso—My capons have names, the one is Alpha, the other Omega, they are the last you will have of me."

From 'Speke, Parrot'

My name is Parrot, a bird of Paradise,

By nature devised of a wondrous kind,

Daintily dieted with divers delicate spice,

Till Euphrates, that flood, driveth me to Inde;

Where men of that country by fortune me find,

And sent me to great ladies of estate;

The Parrot must have an almond or a date:

A cage curiously carven, with silver pin,

Properly painted, to be my coverture;

A mirror of glass, that I may toot therein;

These, maidens full meekly with many a diverse flower,

Freshly they dress and make sweet my bower.

With "Speke Parrot, I pray you" full courteously they say

Parrot "is a goodly bird, a pretty popinjay".

(followed by many more verses)

Sir John **Suckling** 1609-1641

Roos Hall, near Beccles was built in 1588, and bought by his father, also Sir John, in 1600. The father was MP for Dunwich in 1601, and owned property in Norwich. He purchased the manor of Barsham, near Beccles in 1603.

The son John was born at Whitton near Twickenham, he studied at Trinity College, Cambridge from 1623, and in 1627, the same year that he inherited his father's title and estate including land in Lincolnshire, Middlesex and Suffolk , he enrolled at Gray's Inn.

Van Dyck, the leading court painter, known for his portraits of Charles 1 and many courtiers, painted a portrait of Sir John (junior) in 1632, which is in the Frick collection, New York.

Suckling was a renowned card player, it is said that he invented the game of cribbage; he wrote poetry and came to the attention of Charles 1 through his poetry. He also wrote drama, including 'Aglaura' 1637, this is just before theatres were closed by law on 2nd September 1642 - they remained closed for 20 years. Other Cavalier poets contemporary with Suckling include Sir William Davenant, Ben Johnson and Richard Lovelace.

He fought alongside the Marquess of Hamilton at the Battle of Breitenfeld in 1631, a major victory for the Protestants in the Thirty Years War. He accompanied King Charles 1, raising a force at his own expense, on his first Scottish War in 1639. It is said 'he personally acquitted himself as became a soldier and a gentleman'. When the king issued a proclamation that the gentry were to spend more time on their estates, Suckling came to Roos Hall to write poetry and plays.

He went into exile in France in May 1641, there are various accounts of his death, but no record of him after this date. He is buried in a Protestant cemetery in Paris. He did not marry, his cousin Charles Suckling of Woodton inherited the estate, from whom is descended Catherine Suckling, the mother of Lord Nelson.

His poems include 'A Doubt of Martyrdom' and 'Ballade upon a Wedding'.

Roos Hall has the reputation of being one of the most haunted houses in the country. 'Jess of Roos Hall' is an historical novel written by Janet T Sawyer, published in 2007. She has also written 'Watersmeet' and 'A Wooden Leg', part of which is set in Beccles.

A Doubt of Martyrdom

O for some honest lover's ghost,
  Some kind unbodied post
Sent from the shades below!
  I strangely long to know
Whether the nobler chaplets wear
Those that their mistress' scorn did bear
  Or those that were used kindly.

For whatso'er they tell us here
To make those sufferings dear,
  'Twill there, I fear, be found
  That to the being crowned
To have loved alone will not suffice,
Unless we also have been wise
  And have our loves enjoyed.

What posture can we think him in
  That, here unloved, again
  Departs, and's thither gone
Where each sits by his own?

Or how can that Elysium be
Where I my mistress still must see
Circled in other's arms?

For there the judges all are just
  And Sophonisba must
Be his whom she held dear,
  Nor his who loved her here.
The sweet Philoclea, since she died,
Lies by her Pirocles his side,
  Not by Amphialus.

Some bays, perchance, or myrtle bough
For difference crowns the brow
Of those kind souls that were
  The noble martyrs here:
  And if that be the only odds
(As who can tell?), ye kinder gods,
Give me the woman here!

John Suckling 1609-1641

Queen Elizabeth died 1603, succeeded by James 1, followed by Charles 1 in 1625. Oliver Cromwell was MP for Huntingdon in 1628. Parliament dissolved in 1629. Cromwell MP for Cambridge 1640

King Charles 1 executed in 1649, restoration of the monarchy 1660 with Charles 11. The intervening period 1649-1660 English Civil War with Oliver Cromwell becoming Lord-Protector of England.

Reverend Dr. William **Broome** 1689-1745

Broome was born at Haslington, near Crewe, more than 200 miles from where he spent much of his life in south Norfolk. He became accustomed to travelling at an early age, leaving the family farm to further his education at Eton and St John's College, Cambridge, where he was a Greek scholar and nick-named 'the poet'.

He entered the church and became rector of the small village of Stuston near Diss. His is one of five names in the Stuston 1727 poll book. It was here in 1716 that he married a rich widow, Mrs Elizabeth Clarke, they had two daughters and two sons. They died in childhood, with the exception of their youngest son, Charles, who died at 21, whilst an undergraduate at Cambridge, just two years after his father's death.

In 1728, Broome became rector at Pulham, Norfolk and then Eye in Suffolk. He officiated as Chaplain to Lord Charles Cornwallis, his friend and patron, to whom he dedicated his Miscellany of Poems in 1739.

Stuston church

While living at Pulham St Mary, he was employed by Alexander Pope in translating eight books of the Odyssey, for which he was paid £600. He had met Pope in 1714, and worked for him on his translation of Homer's Iliad. The two men corresponded over a twenty year period, but Broome felt he was underpaid, and there was antagonism between them.

Broome died at Bath, and was buried in the abbey church.

(A new rectory was built at Pulham in 1809)

The Cornwallis family lived at Brome Hall, near Eye. Charles Cornwallis's great-grandfather, Frederick, fought for King Charles 1 and followed King Charles 11 into exile (see entry under Richard Cobbold)

William & Mary 1689, Queen Anne 1702-1714, George 1 with Walpole as PM, 1727 George 11, with Pitt as PM.

To a Lady of Thirty

No more let youth its beauty boast,
S——n at thirty reigns a toast,
And, like the Sun as he declines,
More mildly, but more sweetly shines.

The hand of Time alone disarms
Her face of its superfluous charms:
But adds, for every grace resign'd,
A thousand to adorn her mind.

Youth was her too inflaming time;
This, her more habitable clime:
How must she then each heart engage,
Who blooms like youth, is wise in age!

Thus the rich orange-trees produce
At once both ornament and use:
Here opening blossoms we behold,
Their fragrant orbs of ripen'd gold.

William Broome

Daniel **Defoe** 1660-1731, author of Robinson Crusoe, 1719 and seven other novels.

Defoe's 'A Tour through the whole island of Great Britain' 1724-26 includes a passage about Winterton, a village north of Gt Yarmouth on the Norfolk coast "The danger to ships going northwards is, if after passing by Winterton they are taken short with a north-east wind, and cannot put back into the Roads, which very often happens, then they are driven upon the same coast, and embayed just at the latter. The dangers in this place being thus considered, 'tis no wonder, that upon the shore beyond Yarmouth, there is no less than four light-houses kept flaming every single night."

In one of his letters he writes " From High Suffolk I pass'd the Waveney into Norfolk, near the Schole-Inn ; in my passage I saw at Redgrave, (the seat of the family) a most exquisite monument of Sir John Holt, Knight..." He describes the river Waveney "In these parts are also several good market-towns, some in this county and some in the other, as Beccles, Bungay, Harleston, all on the edge of the River Waveney, which parts here the counties of Suffolk and Norfolk. And here in a bye-place, and out of common remark, lies the antient town of Hoxon, famous for being the place where St Edmund was martyr'd, for whom so many cells and shrines have been set up, and monasteries built; and in honour of whom, the famous monastery of St Edmund's Bury above mentioned, was founded, which most people erroneously think was the place where the said murder was committed."

He talks of Southwold, and the "very large and well built church" and goes on to talk about the migration of swallows, " I was some years before at this place, at the latter end of the year (viz.) about the beginning of October, and lodging in a house that looked into the church-yard, I observ'd in the evening an unusual multitude of birds sitting on the leads of the church; curiosity led me to go nearer to see what they were, and I found they were all swallows; that there was such an infinite number that they cover'd the whole roof of the church, and of several houses near, and perhaps might, of more houses which I did not see; this led me to enquire of a grave gentleman whom I saw near me, what the meaning was of such a prodigious multitude of swallows sitting there; 'O SIR, says he, turning towards the sea, you may see the reason, the wind is off sea. I did not seem fully informed by that expression; so he goes on: I perceive, sir, says he, you are a stranger to it; you must then understand first, that this is the season of the year when the swallows, their food here failing, begin to leave us, and return to the country, where-ever it be, from whence I suppose they came; and this being the nearest to the coast of Holland, they come here to embark; this he said smiling a little; and now, sir, says he, the weather being too calm, or the wind contrary, they are waiting for a gale, for they are all wind-bound.' This was more evident to me, when in the morning I found the wind had come about to the north-west in the night, and there was not one swallow to be seen, of near a million, which I believe was there the night before."

1700-1800

Although arduous and expensive, travelling had become easier with the arrival of the stage-coach and we hear of more people taking longer journeys, sometimes even for pleasure. We have a record of those who travelled abroad, Paine and Chateaubriand both went to France and America, Manning as far as China and Scott records in his diary his meeting with Napoleon whilst on the island of Elba, and he also met Chateaubriand in Paris. Other diarists such as Woodforde and Maggs describe Great Yarmouth and Southwold.

Two exceptional women, Barbauld who wrote for children and Bonhote who wrote for the female market - some forty years before Jane Austen - were born within a year of each other, and Agnes Strickland's writings often appeared in periodicals and magazines.

Publication of The Times newspaper began in 1785, but there were earlier newspapers like The Daily Courant, plus general interest magazines such as The Gentleman's Magazine. Literacy was increasing, the ability to read and write allowed men and women to function more effectively in a variety of social contexts. With growing world wide trade, more children - the sons of merchants, bankers, traders, manufacturers and entrepreneurs - attended fee paying schools, indeed Barbauld had set up a boarding school in Palgrave, having been educated at her father's school in Warrington. There were other well established schools such as Botesdale Grammar School, founded in the 1560s, but with a chequered history, plus Eye, Bury, Thetford, Diss, and Bungay. Harleston had several small schools catering for children from outlying villages by offering weekly boarding arrangements. It was as late as 1870 that the first Education Act established free, compulsory and non-religious education for children nationwide.

Some rural people moved to large cities for work, especially during the second half of the century, with the beginnings of the industrial revolution. Cobbold writes about farm labourers impoverished by the enclosure of common land and Crabbe talks of the workhouse and the lives of the underprivileged in his poetry. Gillingwater, wrote about parish workhouses whilst he was overseer of the poor in the town of Harleston.

There are published biographies of Cobbold and Crabbe and the biography of Elizabeth Bonhote is being written by Chris Reeve.

Francis **Blomefield** 1705-1752

Born in Fersfield, educated at Diss and Thetford grammar schools and went on to Caius College, Cambridge. He was ordained in 1727, and became rector at Fersfield, near Diss, a couple of years later. Whilst at Cambridge he was given access to a large collection of materials for the history of Norfolk, and by 1733 he had published 'An Essay towards a topographical history of Norfolk'. He completed his first volume 'History of Norfolk' (which included Diss) by 1739, and a further four volumes-volume 5 includes Earsham and Depwade. He wrote about Norwich and Cambridge, but died from smallpox before completing his work. Blomefield's friend, Charles Parkin carried on his work (volumes 6-11) between 1753 and 1765, and the entire work was printed in London between 1805 and 1810.

Edmund **Gillingwater** 1735 Lowestoft, died Harleston 1813

He is mentioned in Ethel Mann's book 'Old Bungay' as having settled in Harleston in 1761 as a stationer and bookseller and retiring in 1788. He is buried at Redenhall church. In 1790 he published 'An historical account of the ancient town of Lowestoft' and in 1804 'An historical and descriptive account of St. Edmund's, Bury' (priced six shillings) He contributed to a 13 volume publication 'The History of Suffolk'. In 1786 while he was overseer of the poor in Harleston, he published 'An essay on parish workhouses', suggesting improvements. His position of authority is evident in the following news-paper notice,

'HARLESTON, Norfolk, July 7,1788 It being the Practice for Higlers and others to come into and pass through the parish and town of Harleston, with carts and horses, also to drive cattle for the London market, and to remove beasts purchased at the fairs held in Harleston aforesaid, and neighbourhood, on the Lord's day. This is to inform all persons offending herein, that at a meeting of the principal inhabitants, an order was given to the constables and other officers of the said parish, to take the necessary steps for preventing such illegal practices for the future, and also to apprehend and carry before a magistrate, all persons found wandering and begging within the parish of Harleston, aforesaid. EDM. GILLINGWATER, Overseer'

William **Cobbett** 1762-1835

In Cobbett's 'Rural Rides' one chapter is titled 'A ride through Norfolk and Suffolk'. He arrives at Bergh Apton near Norwich on 10th December 1821, and spends a fortnight in the area, describing Beccles as 'a very pretty place, which has watered meadows near it, and is situated amid fine lands'. He enjoys his stay 'in this very fine town of Gt Yarmouth' and before leaving for Norwich on 22nd December writes 'I leave Gt Yarmouth with sentiments of the sincerest regard for all those whom I there saw and conversed with, and with my best wishes for the happiness of all its inhabitants.'

Thomas **Paine** Diss and Thetford 1737-1809

Son of Joseph and Francis, a stay-maker and small farmer of Thetford. Joseph was a Quaker, and took his son to the Meeting House at both Thetford and Diss. Thomas attended the Free Grammar School, Thetford.

Like his father he also worked as a stay-maker, then he sailed on a 'privateer' 'The King of Prussia' at the outbreak of war with France in 1756 (seven years' war 1756-63). He became an excise officer but was dismissed from the service in 1772 in connection with an agitation for an increase of excisemen's pay, written by him, 'The Case of the Officers of Excise' 1772. Two years later he sailed to America, and in 1776 published his pamphlet 'Common Sense', a history of the transactions that had led to the war with England, followed by more pamphlets from 1776-83, called 'The Crisis', encouraging resistance to England. He returned to England in 1787 having held various posts under the American Government. The first part of his 'Rights of Man' was published in 1791, and the second part a year later, in which, years ahead of his time, he makes constructive proposals for provision for the aged poor, family allowances, allowances for the education of the poor, maternity grants, funeral grants, graduated income tax, and limitation of arms by treaty.

With government concern over the political and social upheaval in France, resulting in the French revolution from 1789-99, he was convicted of treason, and fled to France to escape prosecution, where he was warmly received and elected a member of the Convention. In 1793 he published 'The Age of Reason', and returned to America in 1802. This work and his opposition to Washington and the federalists made him unpopular, and he died in New York.

Robert G. Ingersoll 1833-1899, an American lawyer, wrote 'Oration on Thomas Paine', which reads, "He had more brains than looks, more sense than education, more courage than politeness, more strength than polish. He had no veneration for old mistakes, no admiration for ancient lies. He loved the truth for the truth's sake. He saw opposition on every hand, injustice everywhere, hypocrisy at the altar, venality on the bench, tyranny on the throne, and with a splendid courage he espoused the cause of the weak against the strong – of the enslaved many against the entitled few." (Followed by an opinion of the pamphlet 'Common Sense' and letter dated 20/4/1910 from Philadelphia.) (NRO MS 4682)

Paine is included here simply because he had a link with Diss, (one wonders what early events in his life led him to such political activity and revolutionary ideas) and was so influential in the emerging political scene in America.. Much has been written about Thomas Paine, such as the biography 'The Life of Thomas Paine' by the American professor A O Aldridge..

King George 1, 11 and 111. William Pitt, the younger, PM in 1783-1801 and 1804-1806

James **Woodforde** 1740-1803

Woodforde kept a diary for 43 years, starting from the time he went to New College Oxford. He became sub-warden of his college and in 1776 moved to take up the living as vicar at Weston Longueville, in Norfolk. His niece Nancy joined him and lived as his housekeeper and companion until his death. He visited Bungay and Gt Yarmouth, where he stayed at 'The Wrestler's Arms'. Lord Admiral Nelson is said to have drunk at this public house.

He describes his first journey to Weston Longueville in a post-coach and four, arriving at Norwich at 11pm when the city gates were closed. The following day it cost him 'two guineas to take a chaise to Weston' from Norwich. He wrote of his first trip to Gt Yarmouth "We got up pretty early this morning and at 7 o'clock we got into the Yarmouth coach to go to Yarmouth, about 22 miles from Norwich. We breakfasted on the road and got to Yarmouth about 11 o'clock, where we dined and spent the afternoon at the sign of the Wrestlers, kept by one Orton, near to the market place. We each took a Yarmouth coach just big enough for one person and drove down to the Fort, and so on upon the sea coasts and close to the sea, the German Ocean, out of which I drank. We were close to the sea and sometimes the water came up to me. It is a sweet beach, upon the Fort we saw the Porpoises playing in the German Ocean. The tide was going out.

We had a very fine day. After we returned from the sea we went to the Church and saw that, and I heard I think the finest organ I ever did hear. The organist, Mr Chicheley stone blind played on it. Between 3 and 4 pm we got into the same coach and returned to Norwich about 7pm. Yarmouth is a sweet place indeed. The Key (quay) is very fine.

For our breakfast on the road this morning paid 0.1.6.

For our dinner, coaches etc at Yarmouth   paid 0.11.0.

The Yarmouth coaches are very droll things indeed, the wheels very low and directly under the seat, the shafts very clumsy and very long and up in the air. A very small matter will overturn them, being so very narrow and not more that a foot from the ground.

For our fare to Yarmouth and back again each paid 0.6.0.

Gave the coachman - each of us -   0.1.0.

We supped and spent part of the evening at Mr Priest's near the market place, Norwich, with him, his wife and Mrs Davy who seems to be fond of Mr Cooke. She is a very young widow but has two children. We returned to our Inn about 10 o'clock, where we drank a bottle of clarett, this being Cooke's birthday, for which he paid and then we went to bed. We were highly pleased with our Scheme today."

Woodforde went to Yarmouth several times and often took guests, sometimes staying a few days.

After a visit to Bungay in 1786 and again in 1788, "April 3 1786 ...called at Porland (Poringland) and breakfasted. About 12 we went as far as Bungay and there we dined at The Three Tuns, kept by one Utting, very civil people - paid and gave there 0.8.6. Whilst in Bungay we went and saw the old ruins of Bungay Castle - scarce worth seeing- gave there 0.0.6. From Bungay we went on to Beccles about six miles and there we supped and slept at a very good and large inn - The Kings Head - kept by one Hicks, and there we eat some of the finest Colchester Oysters I ever saw.

April 4, we mounted our horses and went on for Southwold about 10 miles and stayed at The Old Swan.

April 5, up at 7 o'clock, went off for Lowestoff, 12 miles, passed a very noble house of Sir Thomas Gooch (Benacre Hall). Lowestoff is a very good town and large, a delightful situation close to the main sea, - on to Yarmouth and stayed at The Angel.

April 6 to Acle." *(I have used Woodforde's spellings)*

July 30 1788 Woodforde went to Bungay, Broome and Ellingham from Norwich.

June 16 1791 he writes that the two sons of Mr and Mrs Custance, Hambleton George and William, his neighbours, are coming home from Palgrave School for the summer holidays, and on July 27 they returned to school by coach from the Kings Head, Norwich. *(see Barbauld below)*

'The Diary of a Country Parson' has been published in five volumes, covering the years 1758 to 1802, the first volume appeared in 1924 and the fifth volume in 1931.

The Angel Inn Gt Yarmouth, demolished 1952

Anna Letitia **Barbauld** 1743-1825

The village of Kibworth in Leicestershire, where Anna was born, was the subject of BBC Four's 'Story of England', presented by Michael Woods in 2016.

John Aiken, her father, was headmaster of the Dissenting Academy in Kibworth Harcourt, and minister at the Presbyterian church. The family lived in a prominent house, which was also a school, in the middle of Kibworth, until 1757 when they moved to Warrington.

Her brother John Aiken, 1747-1822, was a physician, author and dissenter. He settled in Gt Yarmouth in 1784 to practise medicine. Anna and John together published 'Evenings at Home' (1792-6), six volumes of children's prose, and an early example of children's literature, published by Longman & Co. John moved to London in 1792, continuing to write biographies and memoirs.

In 1774 Anna married the Reverend Rochemont Barbauld and they moved to Palgrave, (population about 580 in 1800) a village not far from Diss, where she taught from 1774 until 1787 at a boarding school, managed by her and her husband. This was a large two-winged early Georgian house (demolished 1869) that stood near the south-west edge of the church green, facing the road running to Bury St Edmunds. The school started with eight boarding pupils, paying £25 tuition and board plus two guineas (£2.20p) entrance; by 1776 there were 29 boys, attending two terms from July until Christmas, and from mid January until May. In 1781 there were 41 pupils, coming from East Anglia, Scotland and Ireland to this school where the curriculum stated "intended for any of the Professions, or Trade". Scholars included the first Lord Denman, Lord Chief Justice who drafted the bill that became the Reform Act of 1832.

One of her brother's children, Charles, was adopted by Anna and her husband in 1775, when Charles was just 2 years old. With him in mind, Anna wrote 'Lessons for Children' in 1778, and 'Hymns in Prose for Children' in 1781. The books were printed in large type so that children could read them easily and she was the first writer of children's literature to consider the needs of the child learning to read. Her books were reprinted in England and America throughout the 19th century and translated into other languages.

She wrote poetry, including 'Life! I know not what thou art'; her poem 'Corsica' is a blank verse discussion of political freedom. 'The Mouse's Petition' gives the reader the laboratory animal's point of view as it cries for its freedom from Joseph Priestley the chemist, who knew her father.

She and her husband left the school and travelled in France, returning two years later and settling in Hampstead, where they took pupils. They moved to Stoke Newington in 1802 and she continued to write for 'The Monthly Magazine', 'The

Annual Review' and prefaces for the 50 volume 'The British Novelists' 1810. She reviewed fiction for 'The Monthly Review' from 1809 to 1815, a year after her husband, who had suffered periods of insanity, committed suicide in 1808.

She corresponded with literary critic Elizabeth Montagu, compiler of 'A Dictionary of the English Language' Dr Johnson, bookseller and publisher Joseph Johnson, poet and dramatist Joanna Baillie, poet and writer Hannah More and novelist and playwright Fanny Burney. She died at Stoke Newington. Her adopted son Charles became a doctor and chemist.

Life

Life! I know not what thou art,

But know that thou and I must part;

And when, or how, or where we met,

I own to me's a secret yet.

But this I know, when thou art fled,

Where'er they lay these limbs, this head,

No clod so valueless shall be

As all that then remains of me.

Life! we have been long together,

Through pleasant and through cloudy weather;

'Tis hard to part when friends are dear;

Perhaps will cost a sigh, a tear;—

Then steal away, give little warning,

Choose thine own time;

Say not Good-night, but in some brighter clime

Bid me Good-morning!

(verse 2 omitted)

George 11, 111 and 1V. Battle of Trafalgar 1805, Waterloo 1815. William Pitt, the younger PM from 1783. Anti-slavery movement among British public to end slavery throughout the British Empire.

Barbauld criticised Britain's participation in the Napoleonic Wars in her poem 'Eighteen Hundred and Eleven'. This was met with considerable criticism and she published nothing more after 1812—the year Charles Dickens was born.

James Gowing about 1750

James was a shoemaker, living in Saltgate, Beccles. He was a principal bell-ringer at St. Michael's church and diarist from 1781 to 1830, in which he records "11 June 1802 Raised the bells for young Mr Crowfoot, Doctor, lately married. Brought his wife to town." His uncle, also James, owned 'The Bear and Bells' public house in Beccles from 1755 to 1799. (original diary at Lowestoft record office)

Elizabeth **Bonhote** 1744-1818

Born in Bungay, maiden name Mapes, her father is described as 'Gentleman' – the family were prosperous grocers. She married in 1772 Daniel Bonhote, a solicitor and illegitimate son of the wealthy Vanneck family who owned Heveningham Hall in Suffolk. They had two daughters. Her husband owned Bungay castle in the last decade of the 18th century, and sold it back to the Duke of Norfolk before their move to Bury St Edmunds, where her husband died in 1804.

She wrote poems in praise of the monarchy, and 'Parental Monitor' a series of moral essays 1796, a two-volume book, of which three editions were published, one posthumously in the USA.

'Bungay Castle' 1796, her historical novel, is about the period of the Barons' Wars in the C13th. It is displayed at Bungay Museum.

Some of her at least seven books were published anonymously, such as 'Hortensia' by 'A Lady' in 1769, some under other names, for the female market. Her publishers were Minerva Press, where she was listed as one of their best-selling authors. A contemporary of Anna Barbauld who considered the market for children's books, she was an author ahead of her time in writing for the female market. Elizabeth's second novel, 'The Rambles of Mr Frankly' was translated into German in Leipzig and published in Dublin and Paris.

She died in Bungay and left a shop in the town, along with dwelling houses and a bakery as well as the considerable sum of £3,500 in cash and savings. During her life-time it had been considered 'improper' and 'unladylike' to write as she had done, by other Bungay residents.

At Bungay museum there is a glass cased model of Mrs. Bonhote at her castle, dated 1797.

'Evelina' by Fanny Burney, published anonymously in 1778

Jane Austen's 'Sense & Sensibility' published 1811.

Bronte sisters, 'Charlotte's 'Jane Eyre', Emily's 'Wuthering Heights' and Anne's 'Agnes Grey' published 1847.

Eliza Dreyer, 1773-1849, the daughter of Daniel and Elizabeth Bonhote, married the Rev'd Richard Dreyer, curate of Bungay St. Mary's church and then rector of Thwaite. A year before her death Eliza endowed homes for eight women over the age of 60, the widows of poor Bungay tradesmen. In her will she left sums of money to be invested to provide an income for buying clothing and other necessities for the poor. The almshouses were named after her on Staithe Road, Bungay.

George **Crabbe** 1754-1832 (picture and sample of handwriting at Beccles Museum)

Son of George and Mary nee Lodwick, born at Aldeburgh, Suffolk, his father was a collector of salt duties there. In Ethel Mann's 'Old Bungay' she writes of his 'narrow escape' while he was a scholar and boarder at Bungay Grammar School for a year, "he and several of his school fellows were punished for playing at soldiers by being put into a large dog kennel, known as 'the black hole'. George was the first in, other offenders were crammed on top of him, and George thought he would be suffocated. After he arrived at manhood Crabbe remarked on this affair, 'A minute more, I must have died'."

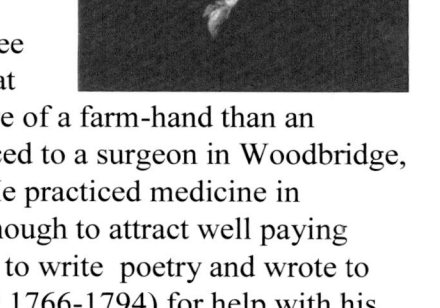

Then he went on to a school in Stowmarket for three years and was apprenticed to a farmer/apothecary at Wickhambrook, Suffolk, where he felt he was more of a farm-hand than an apprentice. From 1771 until 1775 he was apprenticed to a surgeon in Woodbridge, during which time he met Sarah, his future wife. He practiced medicine in Aldeburgh, but his surgeon skills were not good enough to attract well paying patients. He moved to London in 1780, continuing to write poetry and wrote to Edmund Burke (author, philosopher and Whig MP 1766-1794) for help with his literary career, enclosing samples of his work from 'The Library' and 'The Village'. Burke supported Crabbe and helped him to have 'The Library' published.

On Burke's advice Crabbe was ordained in December 1781 and returned to Aldeburgh to take up his position there. He was met with resentment at his rise in social class, and it was through Burke's contacts that Crabbe was appointed chaplain to the Duke of Rutland at Belvoir Castle in Leicestershire. In December, 1783 he married Sarah Elmy at Beccles church, and they lived at Belvoir castle until he took up a curacy at nearby Stathern. Her parents lived in a corner house on the north side of Market Street, Beccles, only a few steps from the church. Sarah and George had two children who survived childhood, George b.1785 and John b.1788.

The family moved to Muston in 1789 and stayed for three years. With the death of one of Sarah's relations followed by her older sister, the family inherited an estate at Parham in Suffolk where they moved in 1792 and remained in the area until 1814, during which time their third son Edmund died at the age of six, and Sarah suffered a 'long and hopeless malady'. Following the death of his wife in 1813 he was given the position of Rector of Trowbridge in Wiltshire by the new Duke of Rutland. His two sons, both curates, moved nearby.

1775 'Inebriety',   1780 'The Candidate'

1781 'The Library',   1783 'The Village'

1807 'The Parish Register', viewed with Crabbe's eye of medical practitioner and clergyman, and a desire to erode sentimental ideas about rural life.

1810 'The Borough', theme of the erection of workhouses, which Crabbe viewed as inhuman, and the life of Peter Grimes, a fisherman.

1813 Sarah died, 5 of their 7 children had died in childhood.

1814 He was appointed vicar of Trowbridge.

1819 'Tales of the Hall' for which he was paid £3,000.

1822 visited Scott in Edinburgh, at Scott's invitation.

1834 collected edition of his works were published posthumously, including 'The Equal Marriage' and 'Silford Hall'.

His younger son John married in 1816 Anna Maria of the Beccles prominent family of Crowfoot, and Crabbe returned to Beccles frequently. He described Beccles as 'that delightful town – the gem of the Waveney'.

He became addicted to opium, first prescribed for attacks of vertigo while he was in Suffolk and his wife was ill. Crabbe died 3/2/1832 in Wiltshire, as reported in the Norfolk Chronicle & Norwich Gazette, dated February 18th 1832, 'At the Rectory, Trowbridge, in his 78th year, the Rev Geo Crabbe LLD., The Celebrated Poet'.

TS Eliot grouped Crabbe with Samuel Johnson and Pope.

Benjamin Britten, whilst in Los Angeles, read some of Crabbe's poetry, and wrote the music for Peter Grimes on his return from the USA. The narrative is based on 'The Borough', the opera is one of the most famous of the 20th century, the location is Aldeburgh in Suffolk. The first performance of the opera was at Sadler's Wells in June 1945.

Known as 'The poet of poverty' the latest biography of Crabbe is by Neil Powell, 'An English Life' published April 2014.

George 11,111 and 1V, Willian 1V 1830, slavery abolished 1833. Crabbe died in the year of the Reform Bill.

Charity

An ardent spirit dwells with Christian Love,

The eagle's vigour in the pitying dove;

'Tis not enough that we with sorrow sigh,

That we the wants of pleading man supply;

That we in sympathy with sufferers feel,

Nor hear a grief without a wish to heal:

Not these suffice – to sickness, pain and woe,

The Christian spirit loves with aid to go;

Will not be sought, waits not for Want to plead,

But seeks the duty – nay, prevents the need;

Her utmost aid to every ill applies,

And plants relief for coming miseries.

From Peter Grimes; The Outcast

...When tides were neap, and, in the sultry day,

Through the tall bounding mud-banks made their way,

Which on each side rose swelling, and below

The dark warm flood ran silently and slow;

There anchoring, Peter chose from man to hide,

There hang his head, and view the lazy tide

In its hot slimy channel slowly glide;

Where the small eels that left the deeper way

For the warm shore, within the shallows play;

Where gaping mussels, left upon the mud,

Slope their slow passage to the fallen flood;- ....   George Crabbe

John **Bransby** 1760-1837

Born in Diss, lived and died in Ipswich, known as a land surveyor, instrument maker and book seller, with premises in King Street, Ipswich and later in Upper Brook Street. He was a Fellow of the Royal Astronomical Society, and wrote

1791 'The use of globes', 1799 'Ipswich Magazine'

1804-15 'Bransby's Suffolk Memorandum books'

1807 'Geography - a general description of parts of the world'

1815 'Ancient & Modern Perambulations of the Liberties of Ipswich'

1817 'An exact delineation of the apparent path of the comet of 1811'

Francois Rene de **Chateaubriand** 1768-1848

Born a few miles from St Malo (north coast of France) at the Chateau de Combourg, the youngest of 10 children, he arrived in London 1793. He had been a captain in the French Army, but travelled to North America in 1791 after the start of the turmoil of the French Revolution.

He was known in Beccles from 1794 to 1799 as Monsieur de Combourg, a political exile from France. He lodged in a house in Saltgate, Beccles, working for a society of antiquaries engaged to decipher old French manuscripts, then worked as a French tutor at a private school for young gentlemen in Blyburgate. Comte de Combourg was the courtesy title given to him as the younger son of the Vicomte de Chateaubriand. He became acquainted with Rev John Ives, rector of St Margaret's Ilketshall, living at the Old House, Bridge St., Bungay, and used one of the rooms to give French lessons to Bungay pupils. He fell in love with their only daughter, Charlotte (see John Barber Scott); the family did not know that he had already married Mlle de la Vigne when he had returned to France from America. He enlightened them, and left for London, returning to France in the service of Napoleon. In 1822, under Louis XV111, he came to London as the French Ambassador at the court of George 1V. He was a noted writer and poet, writing of his travels, novels, his Catholic faith and he translated John Milton's 'Paradise Lost' into French. He is considered to be the model for a generation of Romantic writers. Chateaubriand died in the year the French Republic was proclaimed and is buried on the tiny island of Grand Be, just off the coast near St Malo. His name is still celebrated in the town.

French revolution 1789-95, kingship in France abolished 1792, .Louis XV1 executed 1793. 1796-99 Rise of Napoleon Bonaparte. Bourbons restored in 1814 under Louis XVIII.1848 Louis Philippe abdicated and French Republic proclaimed.

Dorothy & William **Wordsworth,** William, 1770-1850

Their mother died when William was 8, and their father when William was 13. When William left the Lake District for St John's College, Cambridge, Dorothy moved in to their uncle's home, the Rev William Cookson, (later appointed Canon of Windsor) at Forncett St. Peter rectory, south Norfolk in October 1788. She lived there for 5 years and was visited by her brothers Richard, John and Christopher as well as William who visited in the summer of 1789 and the winter of 1790. See William's sonnet *'Sweet was the walk',* written after visiting Norfolk.

William had an affair with Annette Vallon in 1792, but they separated after the birth of their daughter, and to some degree because of the war between France and England. He supported Annette and their daughter Caroline, and gave his daughter a financial settlement when she married. William did not visit his uncle again, such was the uncle's disapproval of the affair.

'Sweet was the walk along the narrow lane

At noon, the bank and hedge-rows all the way

Shagged with wild pale green tufts of fragrant hay,

Caught by the hawthorns from the loaded wain,

Which Age with many a slow stoop strove to gain;

And childhood, seeming still most busy, took

His little rake; with cunning side-long look,

Sauntering to pluck the strawberries wild, unseen.

Now, too, on melancholy's idle dreams

Musing, the lone spot with my soul agrees,

Quiet and dark, for though the thick wove trees

Scarce peeps the curious star till solemn gleams

The clouded moon, and calls me forth to stray

Thro' tall, green, silent woods and ruins gray'.

Thomas **Manning** 1772-1840

Born at Brome, (near Diss) Norfolk, second son of William Manning, who was the rector of Brome and then of Diss from 1811-1857.

Whilst studying mathematics at Gonville and Caius College, Cambridge, Thomas became friends with Charles Lamb, essayist and critic. He coached students at Cambridge, and published his 'Introduction to Arithmetic and Algebra' 1796-1798.

His interest in China and the Chinese language took him to Paris to study, where he met Thomas Paine. Before starting his travels he fitted in a six month study of medicine at Westminster Hospital. He went to Canton on an East India Company boat in 1806; his ambition was to reach the interior of China, but he was denied access. He sailed to Bengal and with one Chinese servant they went through Bhutan and on to Tibet. There, travelling with Chinese soldiers, and treating their ailments he arrived in Lhasa in December 1811, where he met the 9th Dalai Lama, who was then seven years old. He was the first Englishman to enter Lhasa, and to meet the Dalai Lama. Forced to return to Canton, he continued his studies there until his return to England in 1817. Earlier the same year he had reached Peking as a member of a British delegation, but they were forced to leave a few days later.

He kept a journal, the narrative of which was printed by Sir Clements Markham, secretary of the Royal Geographical Society in 1876, 'Narrative of the Mission of George Bogle to Tibet, and of the journey of Thomas Manning to Lhasa'.

The Royal Asiatic Society, London, has acquired Thomas Manning's archive, where he had been honorary Chinese Librarian.

Thomas **Amyot** 1775-1850 (mentioned here as a background to Dr Thomas Amyot)

In 1801 the population of Norwich was about 36,000. Many Huguenots sought refuge away from France between 1680 and 1720, settling in Norwich, Canterbury, London and elsewhere.

Thomas's great-grandfather, a Huguenot, had come to Norwich in 1685. Thomas was born and brought up in Norwich, he married in April 1806, Jane Colman of Norwich, her father was Edward Colman, a surgeon. They had 8 children, two sons and six daughters.

(Colman's mustard works, founded in 1814 by Jeremiah Colman, moved to Carrow Road, Norwich 1856)

Obituary in Norfolk Chronicle of 5/10/1850, states 'eldest son of Peter, (watchmaker, died 1799) a respected inhabitant of St Peter Mancroft…Thomas was a JP for Westminster' He was the Under-Sheriff for Norwich in 1799.

Thomas (senior) was articled to the Norwich firm of Foster and Unthank, and spent a year in London during that time, when he met Mr. Windham, and became his political agent in 1802. Although Windham lost his parliamentary seat in 1802, in 1806, Windham was appointed war and colonial minister and he appointed Amyot as his private secretary, with Amyot moving permanently to London. Amyot published 'Life and Speeches of Mr.Windham' in 1812, two years after Windham's death. This is the only work which he published; he was known as a man of letters solely by his papers printed in The Archaeologica.

(William Windham, 1750-1810, of Felbrigg Hall, Norfolk. MP for Norwich 1784-1802, and other constituencies until his death)

In 1807 he was appointed to the office of Secretary and Registrar of Records in Upper Canada, with permission to act as deputy.

Although he was of Huguenot descent, Amyot was a supporter of Roman Catholic emancipation, and held several important positions in the colonial department of the government. He is listed as Slave Registrar in the list of 'Persons holding situations under the crown in the East India House, Bank of England, The various law, city and all other Public Offices'1845.

He was treasurer of the Society of Antiquaries from 1823 to 1847, he wrote on the historical importance of the Bayeux Tapestry and about King Richard 111. He was a Fellow of the Royal Society, as well as an archaeologist, and one of the founders of the Camden Society. He also wrote about Tewkesbury Abbey.

On the 1841 census he is living at 13, James St. Westminster, with 4 daughters, William, his 20-year old son, a law student, and four servants.

His eldest son, **Dr Thomas E Amyot,** was born 28/1/1817 at Westminster, and lived at Mount St. Diss for the rest of his life, where he was a medical practitioner and a Fellow of the Royal College of Surgeons. He is remembered for doing his medical rounds in a dog-cart, when he was elderly his patients bought him a brougham (a light, four wheeled horse drawn carriage). He married in 1847, Elizabeth, the daughter of the Rev Francis Howes, minor Canon of Norwich.

He had many interests including astronomy, literature, natural history and geology and was one of the first people to write about Hoxne pits. He assisted Canon Greenwell in the discoveries at Grimes Graves, (a prehistoric flint mine near Thetford).

He wrote some verse, 'The legend of Cologne' and 'Oleum Jecons Aselli'(medical term for cod liver oil) which rhymes in the same manner as 'Hiawatha'.

He wrote 'Eglsedene' about the defeat of the Danes by Alfred and the fall and martyrdom of St. Edmund at Hoxne (archived at Suffolk Record Office). He died 19/12/1895, and probate was granted to his younger brother, William Henry Amyot, who by then was a barrister.

An obituary states 'The family, of French Huguenot descent, Thomas Amyot was the great nephew of the celebrated Bishop Jacques Amyot, 1513-1593 of Auxerre, translator of Plutarch and tutor of Charles 1X and Henri 111 of France, came to England at the Revocation of the Edict of Nantes, and settled at Norwich'. Thomas Edward was the great, great grand-son of Thomas, father of Peter Amyot.

Ezekiel **Blomfield** 1778-1818

Born into a poor family in North Walsham, the family moved to Norwich in 1783; he was influenced by reading Barbauld's 'Evenings at Home' 1792-6. (see page 17) He studied Greek, Latin and Hebrew with the Rev S Newton, a non-conformist minister there, and furthered his studies at Homerton Academy in London by means of a scholarship. He became an Independent Minister at Wymondham and married Mary Funnell in 1800, with whom he had eight children. Having written works commissioned by Charles Brightley he went into partnership with Brightley, the printing firm in Bungay, (later Child's and then Clay's) whilst living in Wymondham, but fell into monetary difficulties. The family moved to Wortwell, near Harleston, in 1809. Here he founded the Norfolk & Norwich Auxiliary British and Foreign Bible Society. He frequently lectured on history, and his 'Philosophy of History' was published posthumously, with a memoir, in 1819. He is buried in the grounds of the United Reform church in Wortwell.

John Filby **Childs** 1783-1853   PRINTER

C.Brightly & E.Kinnersly printed works by Ezekiel Blomfield from 1804, including his two-volume 'A general view of the world, Geographical, Historical and Philosophical; on a plan entirely new' of 1807.

Born in Bungay, John's father and grandfather ran a printing business in Bungay from 1795, and after his marriage to Anna Brightly in December 1805, the firm became Brightly & Childs in 1808. Later it became John Childs & Son. They were well known for printing bibles, the company is listed in an 1841 trade directory as bible printers.

John was a nonconformist and was imprisoned in 1836 for refusing to pay church rates. There is a letter from Sir Robert Peel to Childs in Bungay museum.

The firm printed books by Charles Dickens and Edward Fitzgerald.

Their son Charles became the head of the firm and after his death in 1876 the business was bought by Richard Clay & Sons in 1877.

The printing firm of Clays is still established in Bungay and prints over 140 million books a year

John Barber **Scott** 1792-1862

John was born at Bridge House, Bungay and wrote a diary from a very young age which covered events in Bungay. After completing his education he travelled widely, his writings include,

'Journals of a tour of the Rhineland, Switzerland and North Italy' 1816

'An Englishman at Home and Abroad 1792-1828' held at Suffolk Record Office, Lowestoft.

The opening page reads "with some recollection of Napoleon, being extracts from the diaries of J B Scott of Bungay, Suffolk". The book was edited by Ethel Mann, with a foreword by Lilias Rider Haggard. The latter tells the reader that Scott's mother died from scarlet fever when he was 17. Scott studied classics and mathematics at Emmanuel College, Cambridge and promoted education among the poorer classes, being an original supporter of the National Schools in Bungay.

In 1814, while walking in Elba with acquaintances, Napoleon, who had been exiled to Elba, stopped his horse and entourage to speak with Scott and his military companions. We are told Napoleon stayed 22 minutes with them, talking to Scott directly; Scott has transcribed his French conversation in his diary, and then writes "My companions are unanimous in the opinion that he has more the appearance of a clever, crafty priest, than of a hero. I beheld his figure, it is decidedly the reverse of heroic." Scott recalls the death of Napoleon in his diary 11th July 1821.

Sometimes Scott mentions what he has read such as 'Narrative of a Journey to the Interior of China, 1816-17' written by Clarke Abel 1780-1826.

Earlier that year Scott writes from Bath that he has met Crabbe, the poet. "I dined on 27th March at the house of Revd. Humble Ward...through J Woods' uncle Mr Hoare, I met Crabbe the poet and Mrs Schimmelpenninck, the authoress." (Mrs.Schimmelpenninck's cousins were the Gurneys of Earlham Hall Norwich, she remained friends with Catherine Gurney all her life. She was the guest of Anna Barbauld) Scott met Chateaubriand while he was in Paris, "Jan 17th 1823, for the next three months I lodged at the Hotel des Princes, Rue Richelieu....the Vicomte de Chateaubriand, the Minister for Foreign Affairs (to whom I had an introduction through Charlotte Sutton, nee Ives, of Bungay) invited me to one of his grand official soirees, where I met the whole Diplomatic Body of the leading Royalist politicians."

In Scott's 'An Englishman at Home and Abroad' he writes, "6 Aug 1832, David Fisher of the Norfolk and Suffolk Company of Players dies at Dereham aged 73. His name and person are associated with my earliest theatrical amusement. He was born in 1759 and having a fine voice took to the stage as a profession, was very successful and became the proprietor of 15 theatres." (The theatre in Bungay is known as the Fisher Theatre today)

Twenty years later Scott notes the coming of the railway to Bungay, "9 Nov 1852, meet engineer Bruff and others at the King's Head about the railway from Tivetshall to Bungay.

1 June 1859, The Beccles, Woodbridge and Ipswich railway opened and Warrens coach ceases running from Bungay to Harleston.

9 June 1859, Drive to Halesworth and travel for the first time by the newly opened Suffolk railway by Saxmundham and Woodbridge to Ipswich and London, 4.19 to 9 o'clock.

2 Nov 1860, The railway opened from Bungay to Harleston. Travel from the temporary station on the Common from 12.40 to 1 o'clock and back 1.40 to 2.10. Agreeable line and view."

He died at Waveney House, Bungay 10/9/1862, leaving effects of under £50,000.

The Waveney Valley Line railway opened in Bungay in 1860, connecting Bungay to Harleston, Tivetshall, Norwich and London.

There was a large leather tanning industry in Bungay during the C19th with which Scott's wealthy family was associated, making Scott a man of independent means. His father and uncle Samuel imported goods from Russia and employed agents in both Norfolk and Suffolk. The River Waveney was used to transport tanned leather via Beccles to Gt. Yarmouth and from the port to London. By 1932 the river was no longer navigable.

Agnes **Strickland** 1796-1874

Agnes lived at Reydon Hall from 1808. Reydon is a small village near Southwold with 275 inhabitants in 1871. The east wing of Reydon Hall is dated 1682. Her father Thomas, was manager of Greenland Dock at Rotherhithe, where Agnes was born, her mother Elizabeth nee Homer. The family later lived at Thorpe, near Norwich, then Stowe House, near Bungay and he bought Reydon Hall in 1808.

Park Lane Cottage

Second of eight children, 6 girls, 2 boys. Agnes and sister Elizabeth are mentioned in the 1844 White's Directory of Suffolk. After her mother's death in 1864 Reydon Hall was sold and Agnes moved to Park Lane Cottage, Southwold.

She wrote 'The Pilgrims of Walsingham, or 'Tales of the Middle Ages' 1835 and 'Tales and Stories from History' 1837, and in collaboration with her elder sister, Elizabeth, 'Lives of the Queens of England' 1840-8, a new revised edition came out in six volumes in 1864-5 and sold over 11,000 copies. 'Lives of the Queens of Scotland and English Princesses' 1850-9. Her stories appeared in different periodicals such as 'Chambers Miscellany', and a selection, in two volumes, were published in 1865, in 'Old Friends and New Acquaintances'. She wrote verse and prose for magazines like 'Friendship's Offering'. Her other works include more historical biographies and a novel 'How Will it End?', as well as 'On the Ruins of Bungay Castle', 'The Lifeboat', 'The Queen and all Degrees', 'The Lady's Fountain', and 'November'.

She visited John Clare, the poet, in Northampton General Lunatic Asylum in the company of Earl Spencer of Althrop, whose father had been one of Clare's patrons.

Two other sisters, Susanna Moodie and Catharine Parr Traill emigrated to Canada in 1832 and wrote about their pioneer life there. Sarah Strickland married Robert Childs, brother of John Childs and partner of the Bungay printing firm of that name .She is buried at St Edmund, King & Martyr Churchyard, Southwold.

One of her poems

Spring Flowers

Welcome, little buttercups,
Oh, the pretty flowers,
Coming ere the spring-time,
To tell of sunny hours!
While the trees are leafless,
While the fields are bare,
Golden, glossy buttercups,
Spring up here and there.

Welcome, little buttercups,
Welcome, daisies white,
Ye are in my spirit,
Vision'd a delight,
Coming ere the spring-time,
Of sunny hours to tell,
Speaking to our hearts of Him
Who doeth all things well.

Richard **Cobbold** 1797-1877

Born in Ipswich, son of John (a wealthy brewer and banker) and Elizabeth (2nd wife), the youngest but one of 21 children, he was educated at Caius College, Cambridge and entered the church. He moved to Wortham in 1825, where he was the vicar, after his marriage in 1822 to Mary Anne Waller (1801-1876). They had three sons, two of them became clergymen, the youngest was Thomas Spencer Cobbold MD, the celebrated helminthologist (the study of human and animal parasitic worms). He became the rural dean of Hartismere and was chaplain to the Union workhouse, taking no stipend, other than that the children with their master and

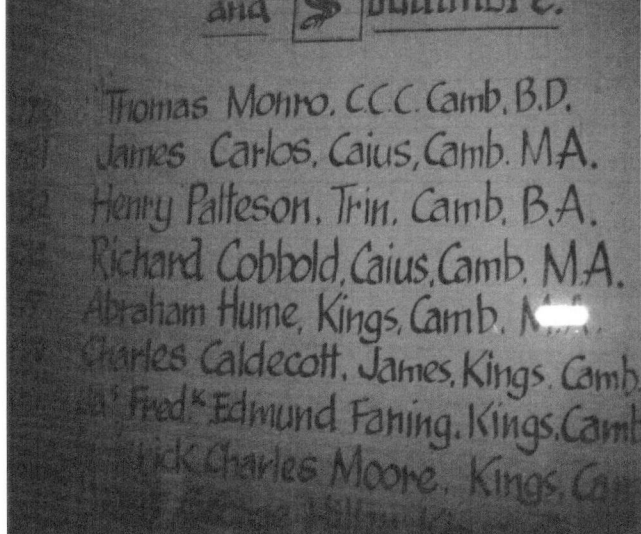

Inside Wortham Church

mistress should attend his Sunday services. He died in Wortham having served the village for 52 years; there is a brass plaque commemorating his life in Wortham church.

During his life at Wortham there was a massive growth in poverty as the population of the country doubled in 50 years. The end of the Napoleonic wars in 1815 brought with it an oversupply of labour and a fall in corn prices. There were poor harvests in 1828 and 1829, followed by some 40 agricultural riots in Suffolk in 1830. With improved methods of agriculture, farm sizes were increased by buying up small holdings and independent small farms. More enclosures took place, particularly of commons, depriving peasants the right to graze a few livestock, gather fuel etc. The Game Laws were introduced, meaning that the taking of game or pheasants' eggs was 'poaching', this had been a customary method of introducing some meat into a meagre diet for the poor. Cobbold comments,

> "A sin it is in man or woman, To steal a goose from off a common;
>
> But he doth sin without excuse, Who steals the common from the goose".

Ipswich Record Office holds four bound volumes by Cobbold, containing written sketches of many of his parishioners with water-colour portraits, written notes on homes and places in Wortham, with pictures. Three of the volumes are spontaneously written, the fourth is dedicated to Lord Stradbroke and has been 'edited' to make it 'respectable'. He recorded the daily lives of his parishioners, now an invaluable source of information about country life then. These records were compiled over a period of years, and he brought them together in 1860 with illustrations of buildings, inns and houses. This was the same year that his younger brother Edward, then rector of Long Melford, died.

His books include, 'A History of Margaret Catchpole: A Suffolk Girl' 1845, for which he is said to have received £1,000

'Mary Anne Wellington: The Soldier's Daughter, Wife and Widow' 1846

'Zenon The Martyr: A Record of the Piety, Patience and Persecution of the Early Christian Nobles' 1847

'A Young Man's Home' 1848

'Freston Tower: A Tale of the Times of Cardinal Wolsey' 1850

'J H Stegall, a Real History of a Suffolk Man' 1851

'Courtland' a novel 1852

'The Biography of A Victorian Village – Wortham' 1860

Norfolk Record Office holds a handwritten book (MS4325) by George Fitt, which includes an article and pictures of Sotterley Hall, Suffolk, plus an introduction as to how Cobbold granted Fitt permission for him to edit Cobbold's manuscript about Scole Inn. As rector of Wortham, Cobbold was familiar with the building and started researching its history in 1855, 200 years after the construction of the Inn. Fitt had written to him about pictures he had of the exterior of Scole Inn and the elaborate carved wooden archway across the road. The rest of the book is Cobbold's own writing, edited by Fitt.

Scole Inn was built in 1655 by James Peck, a merchant and business man from Norwich, a substantial red brick building costing over £1,000. Scole was chosen as it was a trading post situated 20 miles from Norwich, Ipswich, Bury St Edmunds and Thetford, and 30 from Yarmouth. Peck traded in many things, especially in wool. 'The Angel' was the only other hotel, small and inadequate for travellers. Peck bought the land from John Aldham of Shimpling, Lord of the Manor, and employed 70 local labourers and artisans, including one John Fairchild, a carpenter, and another John Fairchild, a wood carver. A huge carved sign was erected across the road, and was said to be the most eminent in the country. The sign tells the story of Diana and Acteon, there are life size figures of animals, including Jonah and the whale and a much embellished sign of 'The White Hart', which was to be the name of the inn. There is a very long description by Cobbold, transcribed by Fitt, who goes on to say "I think the sign was not taken down until after 1795" as it had decayed. In 1870 the irons which held the sign could still be seen in the upper storey brickwork.

A poem about Scole Inn was written by Alexander Brome, (1620-1666) which describes the sign. He was a Royalist poet, author of 'Songs and other poems' dated 1661.

The carved sign at the Scole Inn

The sign was erected on 10th September 1657, and the inn opened on 13th with the wedding of Thomas Peck (nephew of John) of Aspall, Suffolk, and Margaret Welles, daughter of John Welles, minister of the parish – a feast was provided for the Scole residents on the day.

The first landlord was Henry Theobold, who had previously been landlord of 'The Bird in Hand' at Tasburgh, a village 12 miles north of Scole on the main Norwich Road.

Cobbold goes on to tell us that Sir John Cornwallis entertained King Charles 2nd at breakfast at 'The White Hart' on their way to Yarmouth from Thetford. 'The visit of Charles 2nd to Schole Inn. This remarkable record is in the Registry book of the Schole Inn. "King Charles passed through Schole on his progress to Yarmouth, and brake his fast at the White Hart at the charge of the Right Honourable Lord Cornwallis, upon the 27 September in the 23rd year of his reign, anno domini 1671.

It is perfectly correct as to Charles' visit, but exhibits the strange alteration on the part of the Minister of the Parish, calling it the 23rd year of his reign. He means that he never would admit that Cromwell was anything but an Usurper, and that was as soon as Charles 1st was beheaded, Charles 2nd began to reign. Cromwell reigned 11 years of this period, viz 1649 to 1660." (Cromwell died 1658, Charles 2nd restored 1660)

(The Scole church register confirms this, and says that Charles and Cornwallis were accompanied by the Dukes of York, Monmouth and Buckingham, many other nobles and their numerous retinues)

He describes the dreadful road conditions in winter, explaining that the rear coach wheels needed to be 6'6" high and the front wheels 4'6" high to enable the coaches to get through all the fords on the way from Ipswich to Norwich. He also writes about the Balls (dances) held at the Inn, of the Schole Book Society, the Old Schole Fairs and The Road (to Norwich). Cobbold's 91 page handwritten manuscript was written in 1855, and ends with his words 'Scole Inn has certainly been ruined by the Rail.' (trains started running from Norwich to London in 1845)

George Fitt has signed the front page of the book with the date 5th January 1892, giving it to his eldest daughter Sarah C Fitt. He was born in 1809 and in 1881 he was living with his three unmarried daughters and three grandchildren at Windsor Lodge, Town Close Road, Norwich, and is described as a banker's clerk.

Richard Cobbold died just one week after his wife, leaving effects of less than £12,000.

There are books written about the Cobbold family members, see The Cobbold Family Trust website www.cobboldfht.com

Sue Heaser has written 'Cobbold's Tales', see www.sueheaser.com

The Wortham Research Group has written 'Parson and People in a Suffolk Village,

Richard Cobbold's Wortham' edited by David Dymond

'The Biography of a Victorian Village' by Ronald Fletcher covers Wortham and Richard Cobbold's writings of his life there.

In the 1970s the BBC made a film 'In a Country Churchyard' written and presented by Ronald Fletcher, which features Wortham church, the churchyard, many of Cobbold's paintings and some of his writings about his parish.

James **Maggs** 1797-1890

Southwold was a port trading in coal and grain, and much had been done to improve Southwold Harbour in the C18th. The River Blyth was used to transport heavy loads of agricultural produce from the countryside to the port, and carry coal inland. The coming of the railways brought about the decline of coastal and river transport. James Maggs would have witnessed the building and opening in 1879 of the Southwold Railway, a narrow gauge railway linking Southwold to Halesworth, which closely followed the river. It was closed in 1929.

Maggs lived at 20, Park Lane, Southwold, and was a contemporary of Agnes Strickland who lived on the opposite side of Park Lane.

His father, Thomas, died when James was just 2 years old, he and his wife ran The Blue Anchor Inn at Walberswick, where James was born. He was articled to a solicitor Thomas Tuthill, and later taught at Dedham grammar school, and the Grey Coat Hospital School, Westminster. He married Elizabeth Roberts at Walberswick on 16/11/1818 and held important offices in Southwold; he was Coroner 1825-35, census enumerator 1831, first secretary of the Medical Dispensary 1837, Overseer of the Poor 1844, as well as holding other positions.

He wrote 'The Southwold Diary of James Maggs', 1818-1876, two volumes, and was known as a schoolmaster and auctioneer.

Plaque to James Maggs in Park Lane, Southwold

Esther Freud uses the surname Maggs and the Blue Anchor Inn, in her 2015 novel 'Mr Mac and me'

Rachel Lawrence has written 'Southwold River, Georgian life in the Blyth Valley' 1990, in which she mentions James Maggs' diary and an 1842 booklet published under his name 'Handbook to the Port and Shipping of Southwold'.

1800-1900

This familiar thread of writing about their lives, their environment and their concerns, continues to grow, with writers from this period such as Anna Sewell and Rider Haggard gaining worldwide recognition. Baker has left us a vivid factual record of his work in Egypt and beyond in his book 'Ismailia', whereas Haggard used his experiences in South Africa for his adventure novels such as 'She', 'King Solomon's Mines', 'Allan Quatermain', and others which were immensely popular at the time, but now appear very outdated. The works of George Borrow linguist, traveller and friend to many Romany communities have similarly gone out of fashion, but the novels of Conrad, who came to Lowestoft whilst a seaman, continue to intrigue and impress us.

Two military men write of their careers, Alderson, born just three years later than Haggard also went to Africa but his writing concentrates on military matters, Adair saw service in both world wars and published his memoirs in 1986.

The most prolific woman author, Doreen Wallace, wrote about rural education - she was for some time a teacher in Diss - as well as about farming, and was a strong campaigner in 'The Tithe Wars', along with her farmer husband Rowland Rash. Anna Sewell was also a campaigner, the aim of her book 'Black Beauty' - written from the horse's perspective - was to ensure better care and treatment of horses. Ethel Mann edited the diaries of Bungay resident Scott, to which Lilias Haggard wrote the foreword, both were well educated and Lilias had travelled widely with her father.

With the introduction of the 1870 Education Act, all children between the ages of 5 to 12 had to attend school; there was a growth in small fee-paying private schools during the C19th, as well as the establishment of many Sunday schools where the emphasis was on learning to read the bible. Trains, running to Bungay since 1860, would bring national newspapers and new products to the shops and were used to transport people as well as agricultural and manufactured goods away from the town and on to London.

By now paper was being manufactured on an industrial scale, by firms such as Spicers who also supplied commercial and domestic stationery. The fountain pen was patented in 1827, with mass production boosted by the manufacture of good quality pen nibs in Birmingham in the 1850s, they were sold worldwide, with improvements to design and the ink used, increasing their use.

Travelling was made easier with railway stations at market towns and frequent train services. There were no government benefit systems, but towns and villages often had some sort of benevolent society, managed by a committee, which ensured that the needy and sick had basic care. The Harleston Benevolent Society was founded in 1822 and helped many families in practical and financial ways.

Housing and healthcare improved slowly, but in the early 1800s bad harvests after cold winters and heavy rains and an influx of returning soldiers from the Napoleonic wars put a severe strain on some households. Later in his life, and towards the end of the 1800s Rider Haggard travelled the country and wrote in depth about the state of English farming, genuinely seeking an answer to the problem of the poor and working the land. He undertook investigative Royal Commissions on farming and forestry, and was a local magistrate and farmer.

Ann Charlotte **Bartholomew** 1800-1862

Born in Loddon, seven miles from Beccles, the daughter of Arnall Fayermann, she married Walter Turnbull in 1827, and published 'Songs of Azrael' and other poems as Mrs.Turnbull. After Turnbull's death in 1838, she married Valentine Bartholomew, a flower painter, and she began painting still life. She was a founding member of The Society of Female Artists, having petitioned the Royal Society to open its schools to women.

She wrote two plays, 'The Ring' or 'The Farmer's Daughter', 1845, and 'It's only my Aunt', performed at the Marylebone Theatre in 1849.

She died in London, and is buried at Highgate Cemetery.

George Henry **Borrow** 1803-1881

Son of Thomas Borrow and Ann, nee Perfrement, of Huguenot origin, born in a farmhouse at Dumpling Green on the edge of East Dereham, Norfolk.

His father, originally from Cornwall, was an Army recruiting officer; the Napoleonic wars 1796-1815, meant that the family moved to Ireland and many parts of England. George had no consistent schooling until 1813 when he was placed at Edinburgh High School and coming to Norwich in 1816, at Norwich Grammar School. He learnt many languages, Latin, Greek, French, Italian and Spanish and taught himself Danish, Hebrew, Armenian, Welsh and Gaelic. He was articled to a Norwich law firm - Simpson and Rackham, of Tuck's Court, St Giles - in 1819. He completed his apprenticeship and left Norwich in 1824, the same year that his father died. After a spell in London working as a compiler for Sir Richard Phillips, he worked on translations,' Romantic Ballads, translated from the Danish' was printed in 1826. The extent of his travelling is not known, but he was introduced to the British & Foreign Bible Society by Rev 'd Francis Cunningham from Lowestoft, and after learning Manchu in less than six months he was sent to St Petersburg to superintend the publication of the New Testament into the Manchu-Tartar language. From 1835 he worked in Spain and Portugal for the Society for five years. He translated the whole of 'St. Luke' for the Zincali (gypsies in Spain) while living with them in Spain, and found their language to bear marked resemblance to the Romany language. The preface to his book 'The Bible in Spain' is dated 26th November 1842. He was imprisoned twice in Spain for his hostile attitude to the authorities.

Towards the end of his time in Spain he met Mary Clarke, the widow of a naval officer. (Lt. Clarke had died of consumption in 1818, just eight months after their marriage) and they and her daughter, Henrietta Mary, now aged 22, sailed back to England together. They married in London in April 1840. She had inherited from her parents a share of the estate in Oulton Broad, (near Lowestoft) and he completed the purchase with the proceeds from the sale of his works. He allowed gypsies to pitch their tents on his land, befriended them, and was well known for his hospitality. In 1844 in a restless state of mind he travelled to Paris, Vienna, Hungary, Transylvania and Constantinople, fraternizing with the gypsies and making copies of their songs and notes on their dialects. He returned to find great changes in his area, the railway line from Lowestoft to Reedham was constructed, running through the whole length of Borrow's estate. This was carried out by Sir Morton Peto, who became Borrow's neighbour when he moved into Somerleyton Hall, and who was also responsible for major improvements to Lowestoft harbour.

Borrow had mixed with gypsies most of his life, as a boy near Peterborough, at the fairs of Tombland and Mousehold Heath in Norwich, through his friendship with an Irish boy, Murtagh, when the family were in Ireland, and during his travels. He moved to Gt. Yarmouth for a while and completed 'The Romany Rye' there. After a period of decline and poor health he died in his sleep, at his home in Oulton Broad, in 1881.

His books are based on his experiences and travels and include

1841 'The Zincali, or an account of the 'Gypsies in Spain' In a debate in the House of Commons, Sir Robert Peel bestowed a high eulogy upon this work.

1842 'The Bible in Spain'

1851 'Lavengro' (Gypsy word for philologist) The first paragraph of the preface reads *" In the following pages I have endeavoured to describe a dream, partly of study, partly of adventure, in which will be found copious notices of books, and many descriptions of life and manners, some in a very unusual form."*

1857 'The Romany Rye'

1862 'Wild Wales', written after a walking tour of the UK

1874 'Romano Lavo Lil' a vocabulary of the English gypsy language, and considered his most important work, having visited gypsy encampments in London.

(In a local newspaper, on the same page as Borrow's obituary, there is an article about Lowestoft Court, which reads "Jane Smith, one of a gypsy detachment now stationed at Yarmouth was in custody for fortune telling on the beach. Fined 40 shillings or one month in prison", an indication of how original Borrow's writings were, and society's treatment of gypsies at the time)

In 1840 he settled and lived at Oulton Cottage, (now demolished) Oulton Broad, where he became celebrated for his hospitality towards gypsies. Various censuses tell where Borrow is living, eg in the 1851 census, married, lodging at King St. Gt. Yarmouth at home of John Sharman, a confectioner, 47, landed proprietor, with wife Mary, 55, b Beccles and daughter Mary Clarke 37, b. Oulton

1871 census, widower, living 22, Hereford Sq., Chelsea, with 1 servant, 67, occupation described as 'library man'. His wife Mary had died suddenly in 1869, at this address.

1881 census, widower, living Church Lane, Oulton, age 77, landowner. He was buried at Brompton Cemetery, Chelsea

Ivan A W Bunn has written a pamphlet 'George Borrow's Oulton', which was published in 1981 to commemorate the centenary of Borrow's death. (see also entry under Ethel Mann, page 57)

Anna **Sewell** 1820-1878

Although Anna was born in Gt Yarmouth the family moved more than ten times in London and South England and eventually settled at The White House, Old Catton in Norwich from 1867. She spent time at the country home of her grandparents at Buxton, and was known for her love of animals, especially horses. Her mother educated her at home, an accident when she was 14 left her crippled and she turned to writing. She never married, lived with her parents all her life and learnt to ride and drive horses. Anna and her mother Mary were involved with charity work, and while living at Wick in Gloucestershire they founded a Working Men's Evening Institute at which they both taught. She was 51 when she began writing 'Black Beauty', the manuscript was sold to Jarrolds of Norwich, for an outright payment of £40. Her aim, she wrote, 'being to induce kindness, sympathy, and an understanding treatment of horses.' The book, written as an autobiography of the horse, has never been out of print. She died in 1878 and was buried at Lammas Quaker burial ground. (Lammas is between Aylsham and Norwich)

Her mother Mary Sewell, was born at Sutton by the River Deben in Suffolk and became a governess in Essex. She started writing in 1858 for children and the working classes. Her 'Mother's Last Words' is a story in verse of two slum boys, which reached a circulation of millions. John and little Chris are crossing sweepers, their mother dies when they are very young; the long poem begins:-

>The yellow fog lay thick and dim
>
>O'er London city, far and wide;
>
>It filled the spacious parks and squares,
>
>Where noble lords and ladies ride.

Anthony **Trollope** 1815-1882

In what is considered one of Trollope's best novels 'The Way We Live Now' published in 1875, he mentions Bungay as the town where John Crumb lived, Lowestoft as the resort where Paul Montague took Winifred Hurtle, as well as the town of Beccles and the village of Barsham.

Sir Samuel White **Baker** 1821-1893

Born in London to a wealthy family, his father was a West India Company merchant. Samuel was educated in England and studied Civil Engineering in Frankfurt.

He lived at Hedenham Hall, near Bungay probably renting the property, letter at NRO written by him dated April 1860 'Dear Sir, I enclose cheque for £35 for the house'. No addressee. Second letter to Royal Geographical Society, dated 24/11/1867

Hedenham Hall

from Hedenham Hall, signed SB to Sir Roderick, probably Sir Roderick Impey Murchsion, president of the Royal Geographical Society 1862-71.

Explorer and author of books of travel and adventure, his detailed and descriptive hand written journals with coloured sketches are archived at the RGS.

In 1846 he travelled to Ceylon sailing on 'The Earl of Hardwicke', where he established an agricultural settlement, bringing in settlers from England, with their cattle. It was here he wrote in 1853 'Rifle and Hound in Ceylon'. His journal of this time contains 30 plus pages of his hunting with his hounds and the killing of elk, hogs and roe deer.

There is an article in 'The Guardian' dated 19/3/1991, mentioning Baker, entitled 'Cricket – of symbolism, serendipity and Sri Lanka' by David Hopps which reads "..for an archaic blast of empire Nuwara Eluja, nestling below Sri Lanka's highest peak in the central highlands, is hard to beat. It is known as the English village, not least because of its high rainfall, although with its scattered lakeside cottages beneath the stirring hills, it has more the feel of the west coast of Scotland. Samuel Baker, a 19th century explorer is chiefly responsible for this strange colonial legacy. He visited Nuwara Eluja in 1846 to convalesce from malaria. Soon afterwards, his hunting guns, farm animals, English vegetables, and servants followed up the Ramboda Pass. There is a golf course there now."

In 1856 he travelled to Constantinople and on to the Crimea where he superintended the construction of the railway connecting the Danube with the Black Sea until 1859. During this time he met and became friends with Maharaja Duleep Singh (who, from 1863, lived at Elveden near Thetford, moving from Mulgrave Castle, near Whitby)

He travelled by ship to Egypt describing his arrival on 25th April 1861, "Arrived at daylight at Luxor. A miserable, most miserable village, the huts of the present inhabitants being built in with the mighty ruins of ancient Thebes as the swallow fastens her nest of clay upon the grey walls of a ruined abbey. Not much of Luxor is cleared but the rising ground upon which the present village stands is nothing more than the land that nature has herself formed of drifting sand above the ancient city from which peep forth portions of the old buildings, obelisks, statues etc and wherever excavations are made in the mounds of dust and debris fresh buildings are brought to light." He wrote notes in his journal on the use of the sextant, and how to correct the time of a watch by observation of the sun's altitude as he began his expedition to find the source of the Nile. He met with Speke (who had discovered Lake Victoria) and Grant, discovered and named Lake Albert, and was able to demonstrate that the Nile flowed through the lake.

He endured unimaginable hardships, in his journal of 1863 he describes a brutal scene of the capture of a man at Gondokoro – "the men are wolves – there is no other name for them", and Godokoro (government station and trading place, roughly 700 miles south of Khartoum) as "a land of scarcity, you can buy nothing here." He records local words he has learnt, and the fever he suffered as well as appalling conditions "July. Fever again. White ants and rats, robbers and small pox, these are my companions and neighbours." Both of his horses died within two months of each other that year, and all the camels had died by August, with "Relentless wet in all the food" being blamed. In a journal entry of 14th March 1864 he names the lake Albert N'yaya as the second source of the Nile. Later he goes on to say " I shall be truly glad to be once more in civilized society, four years of savagedom among scenes of disgusting brutality make me appreciate the blessings of civilization and thankful that old England is the land of my birth."

He returned to England in 1865, was awarded the Royal Geographical Society gold medal and was knighted in 1866.

In 1869 he accompanied the Prince and Princess of Wales through Egypt and the Nile, and on 3rd June was appointed Governor General of the Equatorial Nile Basin, by Ismail Pacha, the Khedive of Egypt. Baker describes his command as "the first practical step that has been taken to suppress the slave trade of Central Africa. I had been an eye witness to the horrors of the slave trade, which I determined, if possible, to suppress." He goes on to say " to ensure the fulfillment of this difficult enterprise he– Ismail—selected an Englishman with a despotic power such as had never been intimated by a Mohammedan to a Christian." He estimates that at least 50,000 slaves were taken from Central Africa annually. He lists those under his command at the start of the expedition as 800 Egyptian Infantry, 600 Black Infantry and 200 Sagheers Cavalry, in total 1651 men. Also written in his journal are the accounts for provisions for the expedition, copies of letters of engagement of the Chief Medical Officer and copies of letters written in French to Ismail. His personal ADC received £500 pa, the Chief Medical Officer £600 pa and the Chief Engineer £540 pa. The Khedive paid Baker a salary of £10,000 pa. When Baker returned to Cairo in 1873 his position was filled by Colonel Charles George Gordon.

Over a four year period he established a system of administration and permanent government to suppress the slave trade, opened navigation of the great lakes of the Equator, introduced legitimate commerce and protection to the natives. Throughout this time his wife Florence had accompanied him, he rarely mentions her in his journals, but says on 4th June 1869 "Dear Florence and the family arrived by ship."

By 1870 he was frustrated by the corruption of Egyptian officials "thus the Egyptian port official is caught in the act – he had pillaged the country under the pretence of collecting taxes!" In June he writes "I found 7 slaves on board- which I liberated" and on 25th October "liberated 54 slaves from 3 boats." He has written notes on how to manage provisions and supplies in the African climate and there is also a letter from Baker to Livingstone dated February 1873, Baker did not know that Livingstone had been killed in the Congo in January 1870.

His books include,

1853 'The rifle and hound in Ceylon'

1872 'The Nile Tributaries of Abyssinia and the sword hunters of the Hamran Arabs'

1874 'Ismailia' a narrative of his expedition to Central Africa for the suppression of the slave trade, organized by Ismail, Khedive of Egypt

And part 2, with an account of the routes from Wady Halfah to Berber, by the author.

In the same year Sir Samuel gave to St. Peter's church, Hedenham, some of the C19th glass in the north east and south east chancel windows, which depict acts of mercy.

1879 'Cyprus as I saw it'

1890 'Wild beasts and their ways, reminiscences of Europe, Asia, Africa and America'

'The wild tribes of the Soudan' by F L James published 1883, is an account of travel and sport, chiefly in the Base country, and includes a chapter on Khartoum and the Soudan by Sir Samuel Baker, in which he is severely critical of the Gladstone government and its actions in Egypt and the Soudan.

His name is listed under Cambridge University Alumni.

He died at Sandford Orleigh, Newton Abbott, Devon, and is buried at Brompton Cemetery, London, leaving over £61,000 to his family.

The Eastern Daily Press obituary dated 1st January 1894 is very informative,

'For many years past Sir Samuel and his family have spent the winter months in Egypt or India. The deceased knight was 72. Conservative and president of the mid Devon Conservative Club.

MA, FRS, eldest son (Samuel was the third child, his older brother Thomas died at age 12) of the late Mr. Samuel Baker of Lyplatt Park, Glos., born London 8/6/1821, educated at private school and in Germany. He married in 1843, Henrietta, (they had 7 children) daughter of Rev Charles Martin. In 1847 he established an agricultural settlement and sanatorium at Nuwara Eluja in the mountains of Ceylon at 6,200 feet above sea level. At great personal cost, he, together with his brother, conveyed migrants from England, and the best breeds of cattle and sheep, to found the mountain colony. The impulse given by this adventure secured the assistance of the Colonial Office, and with the increasing prosperity of Ceylon, Nuwara Eluja has become a resort of considerable importance, the most recent development being the cultivation of the cinchona plant. In 1854 Mr Baker returned from Ceylon after eight years residence, and at the death of his wife. In 1855 he proceeded to the Crimea, and he was subsequently engaged in Turkey in the organization of the first railway. In 1861 he commenced an enterprise entirely at his own cost for the discovery of the Nile sources, in the hope of meeting the Government expedition, under the command of Capt. Spake, who had started from Zanzibar for the same subject. Having married in 1860, Florence, (she was born in Hungary) daughter of M Finnian Von Sass, he was accompanied throughout the arduous journey by his wife.* Leaving Cairo on 15th April 1861 he reached on June 13th the junction of the Atbara with the Nile. For nearly a year he explored the regions of Abyssinia, whence comes the Blue Nile, and in June 1862 he descended to Khartoum at the junction of the Blue and White Niles, where he organized a party of 96 persons to explore the source of the latter river. They set out in December 1862 and reached Gondokoro in February 1863. Here Mr Baker had the good fortune to meet Capts. Spake and Grant, who had succeeded in reaching Lake Victoria N'yasa, which they believed to be the primary source of the Nile.

Mr. Baker, having resolved to supplement these explorations supplied them with the necessary vessels for the voyage to Khartoum and started from Gondokoro by land March 26th 1863, without interpreter or guide, in defiance of the opposition of the slave hunters, who attempted to bar his progress. The route was first eastward, then nearly south and afterwards turned towards the east. On March 14th, 1864, he came in sight of a great freshwater lake, the 'M'wotan N'aige' until then unknown, which he named the 'Albert N'yasa'. After navigating the lake from N Lat 1 deg 14 min to the exit of the Nile at 2 deg 15 min, he set out on his homeward journey early in April 1864, but owing to illness and the disturbed condition of the country he did not reach Gondokoro until March 23rd 1865. This was the first successful expedition directed from the North in the history of the Nilotic discovery. Mr Baker carried with his vessels all the numerous transport animals, which alone enabled him to proceed from Gondokoro in the absence of native carriers. The Royal Geographical Society awarded him the Victoria Gold Medal on his return to England in 1868. He was created MA by the University of Cambridge and received the honour of knighthood.

Sir Samuel White Baker

In September 1869 he undertook the command of an expedition to Central Africa under the auspices of the Khedive, who placed at his disposal a force of 1500 picked Egyptian troops, and entrusted him for four years with absolute and uncontrolled power of life and death. He undertook to subdue the African wilderness, and to open it to the civilized world, to destroy the slave trade and to establish regular commerce in its place; to open up to civilization those vast African lakes which are the equatorial reservoirs of the Nile, and to add to the kingdom of the Pharaohs the whole of the countries which border on that river.'

*there is romantic speculation about Florence's background, was she a 'white slave girl, destined for the Ottoman Pasha of Vidin'? She married Baker when she was just

17, he was 15 years older than her. Their marriage lasted 34 years. His adventurous life has inspired others to write of his life.

'Imperial Vanities: The adventures of the Baker brothers and Gordon of Khartoum', by Brian Thompson.

'The stolen woman, Florence Baker's extraordinary life from the harem to the heart of Africa', by Pat Shipman.

Wilbur Smith, the writer, in answer to the question "With which historical figure do you most identify? answered "Sir Samuel Baker, African explorer, writer and hunter."

William Aldis **Wright** 1831-1914

Son of George Wright, the Baptist Minister at Beccles from 1822 to 1870. William was educated at Northgate House and the Fauconberge School, Beccles. He became Vice-master of Trinity College, Cambridge and was a Hebrew, Biblical and Shakespearean scholar. He was Secretary to the Committee for the revised Version of the Old Testament and edited 'The Cambridge Shakespeare' from 1863. When not in Cambridge he lived at 12, London Road, Beccles and was a friend, and literary executor, of the Suffolk translator Edward FitzGerald who translated 'The Rubaiyat of Omar Khayyam' from Persian to English.

James Blyth page 59, dedicated his book 'Edward Fitzgerald and Posh' to him in March 1908.

Edward Fitzgerald, 1808-1893 lived at Boulge Hall, near Woodbridge, and lodged at Dunwich every summer through the 1870s, where Henry James stayed in the summer of 1897 and wrote an article 'Old Suffolk' which appeared in 'English Hours' 1905. He was a friend of Thackeray and Tennyson, and financially independent. His friend Edward Byles Cowell had found the manuscript of Omar Khayyam in the Bodleian Library and sent a copy of it to Edward who translated 'The Rubaiyat of Omar Khayyam', C11th Persian, published 1859. He stayed regularly at Geldeston Hall and knew John Childs, the Bungay printer, who printed the second edition of the Rubaiyat, translated by Fitzgerald. Some of Fitzgerald's furniture is on display at Christchurch Mansion museum, Ipswich.

Thomas **Hardy** 1840-1928

Visited Aldeburgh between 1909 and 1912 with his secretary Florence Dugdale at the home of Edward Clodd (banker, writer and anthropologist)

William Wilkie **Collins** 1824-1889

Collins visited Aldeburgh in 1860, arriving by train, seeking background material for his second novel 'No Name' published in 1862.

Collins stayed with friends at the Victoria Hotel in Gt Yarmouth to research scenes for his novel 'Armadale' published in 1866. Here he met Martha Rudd from Winterton, who moved to London in 1868 and lived with him until his death. They had three children.

He entered Lincoln's Inn in 1845 and was called to the Bar in 1851, although he never practiced law. He was introduced to Charles Dickens in 1851 and they became lifelong friends.

Sir Henry Rider **Haggard,** 1856 -1925, born Wood Farm, West Bradenham Hall, Norfolk.   First Boer War 1880-1881, discovery of gold in 1886 in the Transvaal, 2nd Boer War 1899-1902

Eighth of ten children (the sixth of seven sons) of William and Ella, his father an influential country squire, his mother, who had lived in India, wrote poetry, some of which was published. The family lived at West Bradenham Hall, Norfolk, a 400 acre estate where he enjoyed outdoor pursuits with his brothers and was taught to read by his older sister Ella; it was known from an early age that he had a vivid imagination. He went to a day school, followed by a second, in London, but at the age of ten was sent to the Rev H J Graham at Garsington Rectory near Oxford where he made progress and was happy there for about three years. Five of his brothers went to public school, one entered the Navy, Henry was the only son to go to a Grammar School, in Ipswich. Andrew, two years older than Henry, rose to become Lieutenant Colonel, he served in Egypt. While in Akhmim, a town on the east bank of the Nile in upper Egypt, he purchased the mummy of Nesmin and sent it to his brother Henry in London. Andrew's first novel 'Ada Triscott' was published in 1881, and he wrote other adventure stories and poems and articles on sport and travel which appeared in 'Blackwood' and other publications. A younger brother, Edward Arthur, served in Egypt with Andrew from 1884-1886.

An older brother, Alfred, born 1849, went to South Africa, and is mentioned in 'Crown and Charter, The early years of the British South Africa Co.' as being associated with the company.

His father had been a Norfolk JP and magistrate; he died in 1892,and the estate was inherited by Henry's eldest brother, but sold at the end of WW1, (buyer was a timber merchant, and many of the oaks were felled soon after). William sent Henry at the age of 17 to London to be tutored for the Foreign Office examinations, and while in London he became interested in spiritualistic seances and attended several in fashionable homes, which made a lasting impression on him. After 18 months of studying, his father arranged for him to go to South Africa in 1875, as an unpaid secretary to Sir Henry Ernest Gascoyne Bulwer (nephew of Sir Henry Lytton Bulwer). Bulwer was a Norfolk neighbour and friend and had been appointed Lieutenant-Governor of Natal. Henry's time in Africa provided him with much material for his novels, and his first book 'Cetewayo and His White Neighbours' 1882, is an historical record of events in Natal, Zululand and the Transvaal from 1875 to 1881.

He arrived in Cape Town, and after a week at Government House, sailed on to Durban, and then rode by horse-wagon to Pietermaritzburg. His work was to manage Bulwer's HQ, looking after the housekeeping, hiring servants, and arranging the entertaining.

He enjoyed the life, the landscape of Natal and the Zulus themselves, soon learning and speaking their language, and keeping notebooks of his life in Africa. He accompanied Sir Henry Bulwer on long expeditions to meet native chiefs and wrote about a war dance he had witnessed, which appeared in the July 1877 issue of the Gentleman's Magazine as 'A Zulu War Dance'.

In 1877 he was appointed English Clerk to Melmoth Osborn, the Colonial Secretary of the Transvaal, and just two months later he became Master and Registrar of the High Court, which took him on a circuit from Pretoria to the larger cities of the colony, travelling on horseback, with a wagon for the court officials and their provisions.

He built a bungalow in Pretoria with Arthur H D Cochrane "who came to the Transvaal with Mr (afterwards Sir William) Serguent, one of the Crown Agents, who was sent out by the Home Government to investigate its finances. We struck up a close friendship which has endured unimpaired through all the succeeding years. I am thankful to say he is still living, a man of almost exactly my own age" (from 'Allan's Wife') by HRH, dedicated to Cochrane.

Ditchingham House

He witnessed the struggle of the Boers, the Zulus and the British during the six years he was in Africa, becoming an Adjutant and served as a lieutenant of the Pretoria Horse in early 1879. Four months later, after much upheaval and the subjugation of the Zulus, he left his job and Pretoria, sold the bungalow and started ostrich farming with Cochrane, on a 3,000 acre farm about 200 miles from Pretoria.

He returned to England, leaving Cochrane farming, and met Louisa Margitson, a friend of his sister Mary who was staying at West Bradenham, and within a week they were engaged.

She was an orphan and would inherit her family's estate (a 240 acre working farm near Bungay) at Ditchingham the following year. Ditchingham House was built at the end of the eighteenth century and bought by Louisa's grandfather about 1830. Her uncle, William Hartcup, and manager of the estate, opposed Louisa going to South Africa, but the couple married in August 1879,and they sailed for Durban in November 1880.

With the Boers firing on British troops the journey to Hilldrop, the ostrich farm, was hazardous, and by this time Louisa was pregnant. The British forces suffered a decisive defeat nearby, with the Transvaal being lost, just at the time as their son Arthur John (Jock) was born. Cochrane decided to return to England with the Haggards, leaving the farm in the hands of two men who had been working for them, but two years later the venture was wound up.

On their return to England Henry decided to read for the Bar, meaning he would be financially dependent on his wife's estate for three years, so they moved to Norwood, London, enabling Henry to pursue his studies. At the same time he started writing articles of his experiences in Africa, which appeared in 'Macmillan's Magazine' and the 'Gentleman's Magazine'.

The family moved at Christmas time 1882 to Ditchingham House, where Henry continued his studies and his writing. He was called to the Bar in January 1885, so they let Ditchingham House, and settled once more in London, on Gunterstone Road, west Kensington and Henry started work in the chambers of Henry Bargrave Deane, a distant relative.

They had four children, Arthur John (Jock) born May 1881, Sybil Dorothy born March 1884, Agnes Angela born February 1891, and Lilias Margitson born December 1892.

In 1885, having read 'Treasure Island', he resolved to write an adventure story for boys, and within six weeks had written 'King Solomon's Mines', which was published by Cassell's, selling 31,000 copies in England in the first year, their best title for the year, and an excellent source of money for Henry, who had agreed terms of 10% royalty on the published price of the book. Three more books followed that year and 'She' in late 1886, while he was still working in chambers. 'She' and 'King Solomon's Mines' earned him a literary reputation in America as well, and a good income, followed by honorary posts, and his letters to the press became influential.

He visited Egypt in 1887 and was elected to the Savile Club, a meeting place for writers, in the same year. At NRO there is a letter written by his son Jock, dated 3rd October 1887, asking his father when he will be returning from his travelling. He left the Temple and late January 1888 he went on a three month tour of Egypt, a long held dream, but he was homesick for his wife and children and resolved he would take them with him when he next travelled.

By May of that year they returned to Ditchingham House, and Rider began improvements by building large bow windows on three sides, putting in oak paneling and fitting doors from Queen Victoria's yacht.

They retained their London home at Redcliffe Square, near Earls Court, and he visited Iceland in June from which followed 'Eric Brighteyes', considered to be one of his best books. His mother died in December 1889, and he was profoundly affected by this.

Through his connections in the City he met a director of a copper mine in Mexico, a then unexplored region, and they travelled there together with Louisa, arriving first in New York in January 1890, then by train to Mexico City via New Orleans. From Mexico City he journeyed on horseback with his companion Jebb, exploring the Aztec ruins, viewing the native farming methods, inspecting a silver mine and gathering palms and orchids, some of which were shipped back to Ditchingham where they thrived in the greenhouses.

While in Mexico their only son Jock died suddenly of a perforating ulcer after an attack of measles, a devastating blow for both parents, from which Henry never really recovered. (They had left Jock in the care of their close friends, Edmund Gosse and his family) The London house was sold and for two years the family lived at Ditchingham House 'in a very quiet and retired fashion'. The church clock at St. Mary's Ditchingham was installed as a memorial to his son. He paid for the restoration of the south porch of the church, and when Henry died his ashes were laid in the family vault beneath a black marble slab in the chancel.

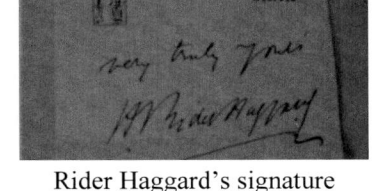

Rider Haggard's signature

He was adopted as Conservative candidate for East Norfolk in 1895, but narrowly lost his campaign to the Liberal politician Sir Robert Price by 198 votes.

Following successful sales of his books Rider purchased Cliff House, later known as Cliff Grange, at Kessingland (near Lowestoft) in 1895, a large, 17 bed-roomed house on the edge of the cliffs. Rider would often cycle the fifteen miles from Ditchingham to Cliff Grange. The property was requisitioned during WW1 for use as an army barracks and Rider lost interest. It was bought by a speculator after

Haggard's death, demolished and a holiday camp built on the 10-acre site.

Having written 'A Farmer's Year' during 1898 in which he reveals the deteriorating way of life for the farmer, between 1901-2 he began an investigation of the English countryside and the state of English farming, which resulted in 'Rural England'. He travelled with his old friend Arthur Cochrane, throughout England, making meticulous records county by county, and produced a detailed survey of the state of agriculture in Britain at that time. In 1903 he produced 'A Gardener's Year', a companion book to 'A Farmer's Year'. Rudyard Kipling wrote to him just before Christmas 1902, saying "In the last week or more the wife and I have been reading 'Rural England' with deep joy."

He visited Canada and the USA inspecting the Salvation Army Colonies - William Booth, founder of the Salvation Army, had set up some rural training stations, where the Army taught men and women from the cities how to work the land, and then he helped them emigrate to the Colonies as farmers. Haggard himself was keen to get people out of the slums and back to the land. He met Theodore Roosevelt, the then newly elected President of the United States, (president 1901-1909) at the White House, and the men developed a lasting friendship. They wrote to each other often, in 1912, Roosevelt writes of their joint aim of getting workers back to the land, Haggard responds saying "The problem then is … the Poor in the Cities, and the answer to it should be, The Poor on the Land, where they would cease to be poor." In 1917 Roosevelt accepted Haggard's dedication in 'Allan Quatermain' – "I shall be delighted to have the Allan Quatermain book dedicated to me…"

In October Roosevelt writes "The book has come and I m very proud of its dedication." During 1917 he expresses his frustration with American politicians, "I am sick at heart …at Wilson's hesitancy…" "We should have been in the war six weeks ago", I did force him to send some troops abroad." (Woodrow Wilson, US president 1913-1921)

Haggard's report of his US and Canada visit were well received in the English press, but no action was taken by the Government. He had written 'Regeneration', published in 1910, a record of Booth's work and the Army's achievements, as well as a clinical and factual picture of slum life. That same year he went to Denmark to look at Danish farming and how they managed to largely feed themselves and export food as well, which he compared starkly to the state of English agriculture. The outcome was 'Rural Denmark and Its Lessons'. Robert Baden-Powell wrote to him on 23rd October 1911, "I am reading with the greatest interest your book 'Rural Denmark and Its Lessons'. I am on the point of starting a farm-school for Boy Scouts on somewhat new lines (as you can see from the prospectus pamphlet which I am sending you) Our aim will be to teach the young farmers the latest methods for making a small mixed farm pay in England and the value of co-operative marketing etc."

(Baden-Powell wrote to Haggard again late 1923 asking Haggard to write an article about the Zulus for the Boy Scout Gazette, 'The Scouter')

Haggard was knighted in 1912, for his work on various commissions studying the state of agriculture and farming, and his proposals for improvement in the 1909 Development Bill. This introduced grants for agriculture and forestry and set out the basis for a system of smallholdings.

Haggard had met Rudyard Kipling in 1889 in London, and they became firm friends, exchanging letters, meeting often, discussing manuscripts and visiting each other's homes. Kipling lost his son in WW1, which brought the men closer. When Haggard was ill in 1925, he wrote to Haggard several times a week.

With the war of 1914-18 there was a huge shortage of labour and he gave up farming in 1916. The stock was sold and the land let in 1919.

In 1917 he moved to St. Leonards in Sussex, near his friend Rudyard Kipling at Burwash. He recorded in his diary of that year '10/9/1917. Today Mr F Levey, Curator of the Castle Museum, Norwich, has been here and has departed with a motor car full of gifts. I have presented to the Corporation all my bound-up manuscripts, with two exceptions, 'Allan Quatermain' which I gave to Charles Longman, and 'Mr Meeson's Will' which I think I gave to my late friend Mr A P Watts. These manuscripts run from about 1882 to 1892… 'the gift of a Norfolk man to Norfolk'… it makes me rather sad to part with them.' and '24th April 1917. Today I held my sale of stock as I am giving up farming. The stock realized between £7-8,000. Farming is a tricky business and who can tell what will happen to it in the future? I have made nothing….but I have gained a vast amount of experience without which I could not have written my works on agriculture'. He reports that the south-east coast was attacked the following day, 25th April 1917, but there is very little in his diaries about himself. He mentions his resignation from the Empire Settlement Committee on 4th February1918, because of ill health and his doctor's orders. He reports on world events during WW1 and government actions, including what is happening in Canada and Russia for example. His comments contrast with his recordings of local life as a JP and the supply of food during wartime, mentioning the watered-down beer, and the effect on morale.

Some of his books include 'Dawn' 1882,'King Solomon's Mines' 1885, 'She' 1887, 'Jess' 1887, 'Allan Quatermain' 1887,'Colonel Quatritch' and 'A Tale of Country Life' both 1888, 'A Farmer's Year' 1889 'Montezuma's Daughter' 1893,'Rural England' 1902, 'A Gardener's Year' 1903, 'Ayesha, or the Return of She' 1905. Collaborated with Andrew Lang (1844 -1912) in 'The World's Desire' 1891. 'Red Eve' 1891, 'Private Diaries' 1914-25. Altogether he wrote 58 novels and seven books on social, agricultural and economic reform.

In poor health Haggard was driven to London from Ditchingham House, and died there on 14th May 1925. A letter dated the following day from Edmund Gosse,17, Hanover Terrace, Regents Park to Lady Haggard says "I can hardly realize yet the loss of so old a friend, always kind and loyal and sympathetic."

His friend Charles Longman, the publisher, wrote to Rudyard Kipling in 1925 about a preface to Haggard's autobiography, asking him to emphasize Haggard's work as a philanthropist and on Royal commissions as well as being a romantic novelist.

His death was remarked upon many years later by the artist, Sir Alfred Munnings, writing from Castle House, Dedham in December 1951 to Haggard's daughter, Lilias, "Dear Miss Haggard, What a book 'The cloak I left'. All part and parcel of your father's work and so sad. I went to his home at Bradenham this summer. Many thanks for all you told me about our hero of yore."

Phoebe Tipple, the grandmother of a friend of the writer of this book, was in service at the time of Haggard living at Ditchingham House, Phoebe lived at Tunbeck Cottage, Alburgh.

Graham Greene wrote an article in 'The New Statesman and Nation' in praise of Haggard's writings.

Commander Mark Cheyne, grandson of Haggard died 2001, owned the estate which has increased to 400 acres.

Bib. 'Rider Haggard, his life and work' by Dr. Morton Cohen 1960, 2nd edition 1968

Obituary Eastern Daily Press dated 15th May 1925

'Death of Sir H Rider Haggard

Author, Traveller, Farmer, Early life in S. Africa. He died in a London nursing home, having been ill for 4 ½ months, the cremation and service in London. In the death of Sir Rider Haggard we record a public loss of the utmost gravity. Aged 69 - one of the most prolific and versatile authors that Norfolk has ever known. 6th son of William Maybohm Rider Haggard (one of the leaders of the movement by which Norwich Castle was acquired and became a museum) he was born 22nd June 1856. His father was a chairman of the Norfolk Quarter Sessions for 40 years, his mother was a poet. Haggard intended for a career in the Foreign Office, but went instead as private secretary to Sir Henry Bulwer on his appointment to Lieutenant Governor of Natal in 1875. In 1876 Haggard accompanied Sir Theophilus Shepstone on his Specialism to the Transvaal. When that country was annexed to the British Empire in 1877 he ran up the Union Jack at its formal hoisting over the new Colony. He was then appointed Master of the High Court in Transvaal – the youngest man to have ever held a master-ship.

He was married in England in 1880 and returned to Africa, where he witnessed our defeat by the Boers at Majuba Hill and at his house 'Hilldrop' the subsequent convention was signed. He returned to England and studied for the Bar and began writing adventure novels.

He was a member of the Dominions Royal Commission for five years. In 1915, in his capacity as special honorary representative of the Royal Colonial Institute, he visited all the self-governing Dominions to arrange with their governments for the after war settlement of soldiers and sailors capable of a landed life in some parts of the Empire. He was elected Vice President of the Royal Colonial Institute..

As a farmer he wrote 'Rural England' and 'A Farmer's Year' which set forth contemporary fact and impression that will for ever serve as a query to publicists and historians. In 'New York Outlet' Theodore Roosevelt wrote of Haggard in 1911, "Rider Haggard is probably most widely known as a novelist, but as a matter of fact, there are few men now writing English whose books on vital sociological questions are of such value as his, and hardly one among his small number who has grasped, as he has grasped, the dangers that beset the future of the English-speaking people and the way these dangers can be met."

Haggard was knighted in 1912 and awarded the KBE in 1919. He was Chairman of the Bungay Bench of Magistrates for many years.

First World War 1914-1918. By 1913 the British Empire was a huge global power, influencing more than 23% of the world.

Haggard wrote the preface to the Norfolk Roll of Honour, Christmas 1919. He reflected "Surely, the lesson they have taught us is that the spirit of Christianity, whose slow, planned murder by the sword of German might brought this unmeasured doom upon the world, should once more be welcomed in the hearts of men and become their guide, since without it nothing awaits us save ruin of body and of soul. That each in his place should remember this, and according to his gift, strive to preach and practice the Divine invocation of 'Peace on earth and goodwill towards men' is the holiest offering which we can make to the memory of those whose names are written in this book; those who died that we might live and that our children might be free."

He was asked to serve on various Government Royal Commissions including those on Afforestation (the birth of the Forestry Commission), Coast Erosion, and the Dominions Royal Commission which, between 1913 and 1918 took him on visits to Australia, New Zealand, South Africa and Canada. He was knighted in 1912. He wrote novels and 'A Farmer's Year', 'Rural England', 'Rural Denmark', 'A Writer's Pilgrimage' (to Cyprus) and 'Regeneration' about the work of the Salvation Army.

His funeral was held in London and he was cremated there. His ashes were interred at Ditchingham and there was a memorial service at Ditchingham church. He gave his Egyptian and Mexico curios to Norwich Castle Museum.'

At his death he left £61,725 to his widow and a nephew.

There is a short 1920 British Pathe film, entitled 'Camera Interviews, Sir R Haggard at Ditchingham' showing him in his garden and study.

The Strand magazine, a monthly magazine begun in 1891, and ceased in March 1950, with a circulation of up to 500,000 in its heyday, has an illustrated report on the curios of Haggard's home, by Harry How.

The mummy of Nesmin which his brother L/Col Andrew Haggard had sent to Rider from Egypt is now held at Liverpool museum.

Another brother, John George, a diplomat, married Agnes Maria Barber, older sister of Margaret Fairless Barber (1869-1901) see page 60

She wrote **'Nunc Dimittis'** a poem in praise of Rider Haggard in 1926, a year after his death.

(There were discussions between Andrew, Joan and Phoebe, children of Agnes and John George, as to what should be done with their mother's collection of poetry, after her death in 1960. 'Selected poems' was published by John Berwick (pseudonym) in Hereford.)

Nunc Dimittis

Dreamer of dreams and weaver of words and phrases,
Man with the teaming brain and the ready pen,
How many times have you told us a tale that raises
Echoes of youth in the hearts of the ancient men?
That sets young pulses aleep and young hearts affire,
For love of the sound of fight, and the World's Desire.

You, when your years are ripe as fruit for falling,
And the sum of your days be gathered into a heap,

When the passionless voice of the Judge of all is calling
    Bidding you render account ere you fall asleep,
    Bidding you tell ere the dust and the dark of Death
    "What of the talent I gave you with your first breath?"

Shall say, "I am humble, I founded nor church nor cottage,
    Nothing have done to profit the wise and the learned,
    Nothing have laid to the sum of science and knowledge.
    Yet I have kindled a little lamp, that burned
    To light the scroll I wrote for the children's eyes,
    To set their feet on a path to a Paradise.

"Where only dragons do wrong, where the knights are fearless
    And wear their lady's glove for a favour fine,
    And all the ladies are young and lovely and peerless
    And tend their hero's hearts and pledge them in wine,
    And marry them next with feasting, and song and laughter
    And, loving them only, are happy for ever after.

"Other tales have I writ that the heavy hearted
    In my house of pleasure might sojourn a little while,
    Other songs have I sung so that souls long parted
    Over the gulf of time might listen and smile.
    Lord, be this pedlar's pack of thought my plea!
    Thus have I wrought with the talent Thou gavest me!"

Joseph **Conrad** 1857-1924

Born in Poland, orphaned by the age of 11 and brought up by an uncle until 1874 when he went to sea, an arrangement made through his uncle's contacts.

Conrad's first arrival in England was at Lowestoft on 10th June 1878, as an apprentice on board the British steamer 'Mavis'. After some sort of disagreement with the captain Conrad left the ship and travelled to London, but his money ran out and he returned to Lowestoft just a month later and signed up with a coastal coal schooner the 'Skimmer of the Sea', in which he made three journeys to Newcastle upon Tyne. In October he sailed to Australia, he worked his way from second mate to master and sailed the world.

A bequest from his uncle allowed him to retire from the sea and pursue his literary career. His works include 'Heart of Darkness', 'Lord Jim', 'The Secret Agent', 'Nostromo,' 'Under Western Eyes', and 'The Shadow Line'.

He died in Canterbury. There is now a pub and restaurant named The Joseph Conrad located on Station Square, Lowestoft.

Brigadier General Sir Edwin Alfred Hervey **Alderson** 1859-1927

Born in Capel St. Mary, Suffolk, his father Edward had served in the Crimean war.

Edwin became a subaltern in the Norfolk militia artillery, and later, with the Royal West Kent Regiment, served in Canada, South Africa and Egypt. He commanded Canadian troops in WW1 in France and Belgium.

He retired in 1920 and spent the last years of his life living on a houseboat on Oulton Broad where he died from a heart attack; he was buried in Oxfordshire.

His wife gave his papers to the nation and they are at the British Library. He had married Alice Mary Sergeant, the daughter of a Northamptonshire vicar in 1884. In the same year he had been awarded a medal from the Royal Humane Society after rescuing a drowning soldier from the river Nile. He wrote

'With the Mounted Infantry and the Mashonaland Field Force' 1896

'The Counter Attack' 1898

'Pink and Scarlet, or Hunting as a School for Soldiering' 1900

'Lessons from 100 notes made in peace and war' 1908

Ethel **Mann** 1861-1947

Ethel would have seen the printing works of John Childs & Son change hands and become R. Clay & Sons Ltd. in 1876, and would have known the Waveney Valley Line railway all her life – the railway closed to passengers in 1953.

The daughter of Edmund and Hestor Norton, her father was a Bungay solicitor. In 1885 she married Robert Mann, Maltster and Merchant. He died in 1924.

The 1901 census states that Ethel, who was born at Regent's Park, London, is living with her husband Robert at Wainford House, Ditchingham, with three daughters and three servants. Robert is a JP for Suffolk and maltster/employer. At the end of her life, as a widow, Ethel lived at 4 Broad St., Bungay. There is an Ethel Mann Road in Bungay. She is buried at nearby Hedenham.

She wrote 'Old Bungay', in which she incorporates many of John Barber Scott's notes, and mentions Abraham Fleming (1552-1607) who was rector of St Pancras from 1593 to 1607 and wrote of 'The Storm and spectacle of the Black Dog'. There is a 1934 edition of 'Old Bungay' in the bookcase cabinet at Bungay Museum, published by London publishers Heath Chrichton. In 'Old Bungay' mention is made of the Nunnery in Bungay, an order of Black Nuns of the Benedictine order. At the time of Edward 1 (1272-1307) there was a Prioress and 15 sisters, by the time of the dissolution there were 11 sisters. There was also a Priory situated between the castle and Holy Trinity church, which was granted to Thomas, Duke of Norfolk in 1538.

Ethel edited 'The Englishman at Home and Abroad 1792-1828' by John Barber Scott , which is on display at Bungay Museum. Through a family connection she had inherited the Scott papers and diaries.

She corresponded, in 1916, with Frank J Farrell, the managing director of a silk factory, who lived in Gt Yarmouth, thanking him for 'particulars of the lectures'. His correspondence concerns the Gypsy Lore Society (founded in 1888), and it seems likely that they were both interested in George Borrow's works. In 1913, Farrell had received a list of Borrow's books and papers for sale from the London book-seller Herbert E Gorfin of Charing Cross Road – see letter below

'Dear Sir, I beg to hand you herewith particulars of the George Borrow items which I had the pleasure of showing you recently and for which the following prices will, I feel convinced, appeal to you as being very reasonable.

The MS alternative reading of the stanza of The Sleeping Bard   £2—net

The parcel of MSS as enumerated below   £63----

For the series of pamphlets, should you decide to take the whole number £3.3s.0 each.

List of George Borrow MSS, The Girl and Boy, 1p4 to 1/2 p notes on fly leaf

Ode to the Cornet   3pp4to.   To Charlemagne   4pp 4to.

Ode to Owen Glendowes   2 1/2pp 4to.

Poem 'The Sun is still in song contending' 1 1/2pp 4to.

The Om Thyme   1p. 4to.   The Birth of Eve   2pp 4to.

Arthur and Guinevar   1 1/2pp 4to.   Eight pieces totalling   17pp 4to.

Pamphlets

Marsk Stig A Ballad   8 vo.

*Letters to his wife   8 vo.

*Finnish Arts or Sir Thor and Damsel Thure   4to.

*The mermaids' prophecy and other songs relating to Queen Dagonas 4to.

*The Tale of Brynuld and Queen Valdemar and His Sisters. Two Ballads   4to.

*Axel Thordson and Fait Valborg A Ballad   4to.

*The Verrier Raven, The Court of Vendel's daughter and other Ballads   4to.

*The Story of Yvashka with the Bear's Ear   4to.

The Serpent Knight and other Ballads   4to.

Of those marked * copies cannot be obtained except from me.' (end of letter)

This list further exemplifies the variety of Borrow's writings.

Charles **Candler** 1863-1931   (There is a Candler's Lane in Harleston)

Born Harleston, the son of John and Ann, his father was a surgeon, and in 1881 the family are living at Redenhall Road, Harleston. Charles became a solicitor and lived in Sussex, although he died at Pulham St. Mary. (Charles's son Edmund (1874-1926) was a widely travelled journalist and novelist and spent much time in India)

Charles wrote 'Notes on the parish of Redenhall with Harleston in the county of Norfolk, compiled chiefly from the records of the town chest' Charles Candler 1896, published by Jarrold & Sons, and 'An Account of the Flowering Plants, Ferns and Allies of Harleston: With a Sketch of the Geology, Climate and Natural Characteristics of the Neighbourhood'1888 by Francis William Galpin and Charles Candler, with an acknowledgement to Rev E A Holmes, Rector of St Margaret's.

(Francis William Galpin 1858-1945, was curate at Redenhall with Harleston in

1883, he also wrote 'Old English Instruments of Music' and 'Music Engraving and Printing', 'The Music of the Sumerians', and was known as a collector of old musical instruments)

James **Blyth** 1864-1933

Born at Thorpe St. Andrews, Norwich, son of William and Hannah. On the 1871 census the family is living at Thorpe, near Norwich. William is a manufacturer, and one of the sons, 21 year old Arthur is a lieutenant in HM 75th regiment, the family employs three servants at Walpole House, Thorpe. Educated at Norwich Grammar School, followed by Corpus Christi College, Cambridge, James became articled to a law firm in Lincoln's Inn. His marriage to Margaret Rebecca Rance, took place in the spring of 1891 in Hampstead, but they divorced in 1896. It is not known why he left London, changed his name from Henry James Catling Clabburn, to his mother's maiden name, and came to live at Fritton near Gt. Yarmouth, by 1901, taking up photography and writing.

He wrote 22 novels between 1906 and 1909, including 'Juicy Joe: A Romance of the Norfolk Marshlands' 1903, 'Celibate Sarah' 1904 and 'Rubina' 1908.

Also published in 1908, by John Long, is 'Edward Fitzgerald and Posh' by James Blyth.('Posh' is Joseph Fletcher a Lowestoft fisherman b. 1838) The book is dedicated to W Aldis Wright MA, Vice-Master of Trinity College, Cambridge March 1908 (see p 45).

(there is a James Blyth, age 47, on the 1911 census, married to Ray Blyth f., b. Bow, London, James listed as author, living at Pakefield, Lowestoft + 1 servant, ditto 1901, but living Fritton St., Fritton) He died in Paddington, London, aged 69.

Henry Reeve Nicholas **Everitt** 1868-1927

Born at Garvestone, Norfolk, lived at Oulton Broad near Lowestoft. He was a solicitor and known as a sportsman and author and is reputed to have spied for the British Government during WW1. A park in Oulton Broad is named after him.

He wrote 'Broadland Sport' 1902, 'British Secret Service during the Great War' 1920, and 'Original Patent Application Number 14687 (or an improvement in the manufacture, make and shape of boots and shoes (Norwich)'

On his death, his friend Howard Hollingsworth (of Bourne & Hollingsworth, the department store in Oxford St., London) bought his estate and gave the land to Lowestoft Borough in his memory, Nicholas Everitt Park.

Margaret Fairless **Barber** 1869-1901

She wrote under the pseudonym of Michael Fairless. Born in Rastrick, Yorkshire, the youngest of three daughters. Her father, a solicitor, died in 1881, and she was sent to relatives in Torquay. She suffered from a spinal condition and poor eyesight, and after training as a nurse and living in London, she eventually settled with her mother in Bungay, who died there 25th October 1890. Her elder sister, Agnes Marion, married John George Haggard, a brother of Henry Rider Haggard.

In 1901 her first book, a religious romance, 'The Gathering of Brother Hilarius' was published and her second book 'The Roadmender', set in the Adur Valley of West Sussex, achieved great success from 1902 onwards, with 31 reprints in 10 years. 'The Grey Brethren', aimed at the younger reader was published in 1905. She died at Hawkhurst in Kent, leaving an estate of £96,221.

In 1920 a biography entitled, 'Michael Fairless, her life and writings' was published by William Scott Palmer and Agnes Marion Haggard.

Virginia **Woolf** 1882-1941

She stayed at Blo' Norton Hall during the summer of 1906 when she wrote 'The journal of Mistress Joan Martyn', and she describes her journey from Diss railway station in her diary. In Richard Mabey's 'Nature Cure' he writes "One evening, free-range reading, I discovered that Virginia Woolf had spent a summer here in 1906, when she was twenty-four years old. She was staying at Blo' Norton Hall, and rode to Diss on her bicycle. She must have passed by our farmhouse. In her journal she described a watery landscape, humming with dragonflies and the marzipan smell of meadowsweet, and confessed to falling into the river ('though a walk in the fen has a singular charm, it is not to be undertaken as a way of getting to places'). 'It would need', she wrote, ' a careful and skillful brush to give a picture of this strange, grey-green, undulating, dreaming, philosophizing and remembering land.' It's an arresting vision: Virginia Woolf as deep ecologist and premonitory river-dipper. But her labile imagination could hardly have failed to chime with this mercurial water-scape." (quoted with kind permission of Richard Mabey)

Arthur Mitchell **Ransome** 1884-1967

Son of Cyril and Edith Rachel nee Boulton, Arthur was born in Leeds, Arthur's father was Professor of History at what is now the University of Leeds. The Ransomes originally came from East Anglia, the brother of Arthur's great-great-grandfather started the Ipswich engineering firm of Ransome and Rapier.

The 1891 census shows the family living at Balmoral Terrace, Headingley, Leeds, with a younger sister Cecily and younger brother Geoffrey plus three servants.

On the 1901 census, Arthur is a boarder at Rugby School, aged 17.

Arthur married Ivy Constance Walker 13/3/1909 at West Kensington, they had one daughter, Tabitha, but the marriage was unsuccessful and Arthur went to Russia where he worked as a foreign correspondent for the Manchester Guardian in Moscow. Here he met Evgenia, who was Trotsky's secretary. Arthur managed to bring her to England and they were married in 1924. They had sailed on the Broads before, and in 1933 they sailed from Gt. Yarmouth to Breydon Water and on to Oulton Broad and Beccles. They came back in 1934 to visit all the places that feature in Coot Club, and sailed on the River Waveney from Yarmouth to Beccles.

Many of his books are set in the Lake District, The Norfolk Broads and the River Orwell with Pin Mill, Suffolk. See 'Arthur Ransome's East Anglia, A search for coots, swallows and amazons' by Roger Wardale.

He is buried in St Paul Churchyard, Susland, Cumbria, his wife died eight years later and shares his burial place.

Lilias Rider **Haggard** 1892-1968

Youngest daughter of Sir Henry, she was awarded the MBE for her nursing duties in WW1. She travelled with her father in Egypt and South Africa, and with her mother to South America in 1914, and to Rio de Janeiro Brazil in 1926, returning from Beunos Aires three months later.

After her father's death in 1925 she lived at 'Bath House' on the Ditchingham Estate, overlooking Outney Common. She was a member of Norfolk County Council from 1949 to 1952. In 1953 she was elected President of the Norfolk Rural Craftsmen's Guild.

She died at Ditchingham, and is buried next to her younger brother Jock in St Mary's Churchyard, Ditchingham.

'I walked by night' 1935-written from the manuscript of an autobiography of local poacher Fred Rolfe*, and illustrated by Edward Seago.

'The Rabbit Skin Cap' 1939 - the biography of unemployed George Baldry and his hardships and efforts to find work. Both can be seen in manuscript form at Bungay Museum, plus Rolfe's fold up gun on display.

Her book 'Norfolk Life' 1943, is based on columns she wrote for the Eastern Daily Press and was edited by Henry Williamson.

In her 'Norfolk Notebook' 1947, she writes, 'He (Rudyard Kipling) and my father were firm friends. … To those who knew Kipling, and guessed at the depths and humanity of his genius, comes the conviction the world will never see his like again. He and my father were more than friends, they had that spiritual link which knits some outstanding natures.'

She wrote 'Country Scrapbook' 1950 and 'The Cloak That I Left' 1951 – a biography of her father, including the sale of Bradenham Hall in 1918, which had been managed by Rider's eldest brother William. She also wrote the Foreword to John Barber Scott's 'The Englishman at Home and Abroad' 1920.

* Charlotte Paton has written 'The King of the Norfolk Poachers', published 2009, about the life of Fred Rolfe. She has researched Fred's life, and in her words 'The true story of Rolfe's life is just as remarkable as his original tale, although it was embroidered and he glossed over some of his less pleasant actions, particularly where his wives were concerned.'

A biography of Lilias has been written by Victoria Manthorpe, entitled 'Lilian Rider Haggard: Countrywoman' (Poppyland Publishing 2015)

Henry **Williamson** 1895-1977

Fought in WW1, commissioned into the Machine Gun Corps, and served in France. His paternal grandmother was German and he was greatly affected by the pointlessness of war. His WW1 experiences made him determined that Britain and Germany should never go to war again and he opposed WW2. He and T E Lawrence were friends, Williamson began writing in 1921, moved to Devon, and married Loetitia Herbert in 1925 – they had six children. 'Tarka the Otter' was published in 1927 and Williamson won the Hawthornden Prize for it in 1928. In 1936 he bought a farm in Stiffkey, Norfolk and moved there with his family, which he wrote about in 'The story of a Norfolk Farm' 1941. The family left the farm in 1946 and Henry went to live alone at Georgeham in Devon. He edited Lilias Rider Haggard's 'Norfolk Life' published 1943. His sister lived at Ditchingham. He wrote over fifty books, in 1951 the first of 15 volumes of 'A chronicle of ancient sunlight' was published.

'Tarka the Otter', in part about the cruelty of otter hunting, was made into a film, and Williamson died on the day the death of Tarka was being filmed. His obituary in 'The Times' 15/8/1977, describes him as 'novelist and writer of nature stories'. There is a Henry Williamson Society, which was founded in 1980.

Major General Sir Allan Adair 1897-1988

Born in London, educated at Harrow school from 1912 to 1916. He fought in WW1, having been made a probationary Second Lieutenant in the 5th Battalion of the Grenadier Guards in 1916. He served in France and Belgium, and was awarded the Military Cross for 'conspicuous gallantry' in December 1918.

He continued to serve in the Army, had been promoted to Lieutenant Colonel by 1940 and was Commander of the Guards Armoured Division from 1942. He took part in Operation Overlord (D-Day landings), then advanced into Belgium where his division liberated Brussels. The division was in Germany at the time of the German surrender in May 1945. He received many honours and retired from active service in 1947.

In 1986 his memoirs were published 'A Guards' General: the memoirs of Major General Sir Allan Adair'.

He married Enid Ward in 1919, they had two sons and three daughters. He inherited Flixton Hall in 1949, but it was sold in 1950 and demolished in 1952. The house had been built by Sir Nicholas Tasburgh in the reign of James 1 and was partly destroyed by fire in 1846, leaving the outer walls, and the house was subsequently rebuilt.

Military Cross

He lived at the village of Raveningham, just 10 miles north east of Flixton thereafter.

_{Queen Victoria died January 1901 and was succeeded by Edward V1, followed by George V from 1910 until 1936. Adair would have experienced great advances in warfare, including the transformation of the Royal Flying Corps to the Royal Air Force in 1918.}

Doreen Wallace 1897-1989

Born in Cumberland, educated at Malvern and Somerville College, Oxford, where she published a book of verse, and knew Dorothy L Sayers and Vera Brittain. She lived in Diss and taught at the Grammar School until she married Rowland Rash in 1922 when she moved to Wortham Manor. They had three children. (Richard Cobbold wrote about the house and would have known the Betts family who had lived there)

The two main themes of her writing are education and farming, and she actively campaigned against the imposition of tithes during the agricultural depression of the 1930s, saying, "In the 1930s my husband and I, along with A G Mobbs, organized the tithe war which has freed the land of England from a tax imposed by the established church." The stock on her two farms was impounded in 1934, this was followed by a siege at Wortham Manor, confrontation with local Blackshirts and bankruptcy in 1939.

(In 1936 a Tithe Bill was introduced which made the tithe rent charge a personal debt. If a farmer resisted paying tithes, goods could be seized and sold in lieu. There is a painting depicting such a scene at the Museum of East Anglian Rural Life, which includes Rowland Rash and A G Mobbs, who was chairman of the Suffolk Tithe-Payers Association) There is a stone memorial to the Tithe War in Wortham.

The tithes were finally abolished in 1977. She returned to live in Diss in 1978, where she died, having written factual books as well as 48 novels, some of which are:-

'A Little Learning' 1931

'Barnham Rectory' 1934

'In a Green Shade' 1950

'Sons of Gentlemen' 1953

'The Millpond' 1966

'Ashbury People' 1968

'Landscape with Figures' 1976

And factual books such as

'Eastern England and the Fens' 1939

'How to grow food: A wartime guide' 1940

'English Lakeland' 1942

There is a biography, 'Doreen Wallace 1897-1989, writer and social campaigner' by June Shepherd, published 1999.

Part of Norfolk & Suffolk Journal 'One Woman's World'

A review, written by John Betjeman, of 'Root of Evil' dated 21st March 1952 reads "Root of Evil is a modern morality. Doreen Wallace always writes moralities. Her books are quite on their own and I like them very much. Former novels have been about poor country people trying to ride above their circumstances and generally failing to do so...."

She was a water-colour landscape painter and a member of the Ipswich Art Club 1924-28 and 1958-65, and exhibited her pictures from Wortham Manor and with the Norfolk & Norwich Art Circle.

1900-2019

The mechanization of almost every process affecting our lives from changes in farming methods, the use of the motor car, electricity supply and sewage systems eventually coming in the mid 1950s to our villages, printing and publishing, photography, transport including air travel - the effects of all this productivity ring loud and clear with many writers. Adrian Bell, with brushstrokes of his pen evokes the hardships of the farm labourer and of his own working life as a farmer and quietly informs us of how farming has been transformed in the C20th. Adrian Bloom, the horticulturalist, wants people to know about the conifers and garden shrubs he grew so successfully, and Philip Wayre is keen to share his passion for wild life including otters, he even had a five minute lunch time slot on Anglia TV as early as 1959.

Some writers have been involved in education, the University of East Anglia, founded in 1963 in Norwich, is where Malcolm Bradbury, with Angus Wilson, established the UK's first creative writing course, which has grown to international recognition. W G Sebald, from Bavaria worked here, he wrote in his native German and his books have been translated by Anthea Bell, the daughter of Adrian Bell. Another writer from abroad who settled in this area is Elizabeth Smart from Canada who lived at Flixton. Lindsay Clarke, George Evans, Roger Deakin, Richard Mabey all taught for a while, their interest and concerns about how modern life was affecting not just our local area, but the entire planet have taken different, and sometimes influential paths; Richard is often consulted about environmental matters by the BBC. Roger was involved with the early days of Friends of the Earth. Ian Carstairs, now living in Harleston, describes with great clarity his 10 year involvement in the Yorkshire River Derwent campaign when a river was legally defined for the very first time, and how this would affect the future use and development of that river.

George Orwell lived at his parents' home in Southwold for a while, a fact now proclaimed by the installation of a large portrait of him on the pier; ironically he did not write any of his novels here and it is said that he did not like Southwold. Arnold Wesker, the playwright, was also a visitor to the Waveney valley through family connections, his wife's parents lived at Beck Farm, Redenhall near Harleston.

Elizabeth Jane Howard moved from London to Bungay, Diane Athill spent childhood times at Ditchingham Hall and frequently visited Bungay, Christopher Reeve has written many books about the town that is his home. Elaine Murphy, after a career in medicine has researched and written about two important houses in the valley, adding to our knowledge and understanding of the area. Ian Mclachlan tells us much of the history of the USAF during its war years in East Anglia. Both

Louis de Bernieres and Terence Blacker are musicians as well as very successful novelists; they and others before them have chosen this quiet, gentle and tranquil few miles, with its modest slow moving river at its heart, as a place for their home.

In the 1950s and 60s improved paper production ensured supply and choice. Ballpoint pens became readily available following the patented design of the Biro brothers. By the end of the 1990s most people owned a home computer to write and communicate which has revolutionized the printing and publishing business.

Eugene **Ulph** 1900-1971

Uncle of John Nursey, who wrote 'Time Remembered, a selection of the writings of Eugene Ulph' Eugene was brought up in a marsh cottage on Beccles common where his grandfather was the Corporation marshman. He was the Beccles Borough Archivist 1948-1971 and chairman of the Beccles Historical Society for 25 years. He began and built up the collection which became the basis for Beccles Museum.

Eugene wrote regular articles in the weekly Waveney Chronicle, and also for the EDP.

Adrian Hanbury **Bell** 1901-1980

Born in Manchester to Robert and Frances (Fanny). Robert was news editor of The Observer, a socialist and republican, Fanny an artist. The family moved to London and Adrian describes his earliest childhood memories in his book 'The Balcony'. Adrian, adored by his mother was the eldest of three children. Francis, his brother, and he attended Uppingham public school, where earlier generations of the family had been educated, after prep school in Eastbourne. Their sister, Stephanie went to Ravens Croft School, also in Eastbourne; her mother never wrote to her while she was there.

At 19, Adrian left London for Suffolk to learn about farming, living for a year with Suffolk farmer, Vic Savage as his mentor, at Hundon Great Lodge in Suffolk. A year later his father bought nearby Stephenson's Farm for Adrian – 35 acres and thatched farmhouse for £850 plus £200 for stock and machinery, with Adrian living and working there from autumn 1921.

'Corduroy' 1930, 'Silver Ley' 1931, 'The Cherry Tree' 1932, are a trilogy of his early farming years and he has written over 20 other books on the countryside, describing the transition from hand labour to mechanized farm practices, frequently portraying old skills poetically and with respect for the countryman who had barely moved from his village all his life.

Adrian married Marjorie Hilda Gibson in January 1931 at Ealing, London. Marjorie, the fourth of five siblings, was born in the Transvaal, South Africa in 1908, but by 1911 she and her family were living in Canterbury, England.

Adrian and Marjorie's children are Martin Bell, former MP and Anthea, translator from French, German and Danish to English.

Bell lived within a mile of John Nash, (the artist, who illustrated 'Men and the Fields') near the river Stour in the 1930s. Ronald Blythe, who met Adrian in his later years, described this book as "among the best rural literature of the 20th century."

Bell wrote of his book "Men and the Fields is an account of this home and this 'family' of neighbours, near to which I was born and where I have dwelt most of my life, looking at these very fields and some of the descendants of these very men, women and children. John Constable walked through it many a time, going to see his uncles and aunts, often sketching all the way. And I would often sit on a bank while John (Nash) drew trees and ponds."

He was the first compiler of The Times crossword in 1930 and went on to compile more than 3,000 crosswords over a 50 year period. Adrian Bell received five guineas for each crossword.

Crosswords first appeared in 'The New York Sunday World' on 21st December 1913. Most American daily papers featured a crossword soon after. In England the first crossword appeared in 'The Sunday Express' in 1924, followed by 'The Daily Telegraph' 30th July 1925, the Manchester Guardian in 1929 and The Times in 1930.

He published a volume of poems in 1935, and his regular pieces for the Eastern Daily Press, titled 'Countryman's Notebook' ran for 30 years from 1950.

He moved to farm at Redisham near Beccles and became a friend of Edmund Blunden and Alfred Munnings. Bell and Munnings were joint guest speakers at the Bungay Town Dinner of 1953 - Queen Elizabeth 11's Coronation Year.

He retired to 19, Northgate St., Beccles. His 'Street in Suffolk' is based on Northgate Street. He was President of the Beccles Society after Sir Charles Auchinleck.

He is buried at Barsham churchyard, where there is a memorial near the south porch. His son Martin wrote 'Notebook for a Countryman' in September 1980,

"If we buried him privately, it was not that we wished to be exclusive in our grief. But he had always a certain dislike of crowds: and a man has no reason to shift his opinions, just because he's dead.

So there were no crowds that day in Barsham Churchyard, just some twenty people, family and some friends as close, to honour the passing of a good and gracious man.

The churchyard was sunlit and windswept, and the service was held entirely at the graveside. ("He always preferred it out of doors" said a grand-daughter aged seven) The words were the old ones, from the book of Common Prayer. He had wanted no new-fangled service nor no new-fangled anything.

He was, we were reminded, an essentially old-fangled man (which is not to say reactionary, or even necessarily conservative) and we sensed that we had with us at the graveside, in spirit, the community of the old-fangled: his legion of admirers both known and unknown, people whose feelings he expressed by expressing his own, "Eastern Daily Press " readers mostly who every Saturday for thirty years turned first to the centre page for a saner view of the world than that afforded by the furore of the front page. (I write as one who lives by such furore and not at all to disparage it.)

He was a man of ambitious notions, but few wants. One wish that he had expressed, however was to end his days in a quiet corner of a Suffolk churchyard. He has just such a pastoral resting place. It is overlooked from one angle by the church tower, and from another by the rectory where Nelson's mother was born. He is surrounded by his neighbours' ancestors, and far enough from the main road - out of earshot even of the living - to be indifferent to its thunderings......

Out in the Glebe Meadow, a Belgian visitor at his easel was painting that churchyard scene. It is the quintessence of England the foreigner looks for, but does not so easily find. We assured him, in the most serviceable French that we could muster that he was very welcome to stay. My father would only have been delighted to have an artist in attendance.

All of us there - the painter, the thatcher, the priest, the mourners - we were a lot so it seemed, like figures from an English landscape. But it was a scene also with such themes and resonances - of death and decay, of renewal and survival - that there was only one artist I knew who could really do justice to it. He was an artist in words, and we were burying him." 13/9/1980

George **Orwell** 1903-1950, pen name of Eric Arthur Blair

Son of Richard Walmesley Blair and Ida Mabel, nee Limouzin, born Montihari, Bihar, India. Richard worked in the opium department of the Civil Service, Ida came back to England in 1904 with Eric, with her husband returning in 1907 for 3 months. On the 1911 census George lived at 22, Western Road, Henley-on-Thames, with mother, sister Avril, aged 3 and two servants.

After school in Eastbourne, where began his life long friendship with Cyril Connolly, (literary critic and writer) he went for a term to Wellington College, and then to Eton as a King's Scholar. Family finances were not adequate to finance Eric at Oxbridge, resulting in Eric joining the Indian Imperial Police in 1922, serving at Hatha and Moulmein in Burma. He came to hate imperialism and left the police in 1927, returning to England to become a writer. He lived in Paris in the spring of 1928, where he had an aunt living, and had to take on menial jobs to earn a living.

From later in 1929 he lived for some time at Southwold, at the home of his parents at 3 Queen St., and later 36 High St. see chapter 8 ' A Provincial Life' in Michael Shelden's biography, in which his sister Avril states "Eric loathed Southwold." There is now a large portrait of him on Southwold pier.

Just before publication of his 'Down and Out in Paris and London' in 1933 Eric had suggested four pseudonyms to his literary agent Leonard Moore, one of which was George Orwell, which was adopted as his *nom de plume*. He had been introduced to Leonard by Mabel Fierz, a Southwold friend who lived most of the time in Hampstead.

1934, 'Burmese Days'   1935, 'A Clergyman's Daughter'

1936, 'Keep the Aspidistra Flying'   1937, 'The Road to Wigan Pier'

1938, 'Homage to Catalonia'   1939, 'Coming up for Air'

1940, 'Inside the Whale'   1941,'The Lion and the Unicorn'

1945, 'Animal Farm' (secured Orwell's international reputation)   1946, 'Critical Essays'

1947, 'The English People'   1949, 'Nineteen Eighty-Four'

He married Eileen O'Shaughnessy at Royston in the early summer 1936 before going to Spain in December 1936 as a fighter for the Republican side in the Spanish Civil War believing that 'fascism would be morally calamitous.' His wife joined him in Spain later. He was shot through the neck and nearly killed, and they lived in Morocco for six months so he could recover. He returned to England disillusioned with Spain and joined the Independent Labour Party, an extreme left-wing ideological group with pacifist principles.

In 1940 they moved to 18 Dorset Chambers, Chagford St., Marylebone, and he joined the Home Guard for the duration of the war, poor health having exempted him from the army. He and Eileen adopted a baby boy, born May 1944, Richard Horatio Blair. Eric was taken ill while he was in Cologne in the spring of 1945, while he was there Eileen died in Newcastle during an operation to remove a tumour – she had not told her husband about her illness.

He lived on the island of Jura with his son, to give Richard the chance to grow up in a natural environment. Eric died from tuberculosis aged 46, and was frequently in hospital for his last three years. He married Sonia Brownell in October 1949. Richard was brought up by an aunt after his father's death. Orwell died in London and was buried at Sutton Courtenay, Oxfordshire.

Sir John **Betjeman** 1906-1984,CBE

Son of Ernest and Bessie, Ernest was a manufacturing cabinet maker.

1911 census, family living at 31, West Hill, Highgate, with two servants.

He married Penelope Valentine Hester Chetwode in the summer of 1933 in Edmonton and was appointed Poet Laureate in 1972.

Sir John visited Diss by train in 1963 while making a series of programmes for the BBC on English market towns, see 'A mind's journey to Diss' addressed to Mary Wilson, page 74. He became involved with the preservation of Diss and was Patron of the Diss Society.

His visit to King's Lynn by train via the royal station at Wolferton was recorded for a BBC tv programme, and he wrote about the Suffolk town 'Felixstowe, or the last of her order' in his poem of that title.

He is buried at St Enedoc Churchyard, Trebetherick, Cornwall, his gravestone says John Betjeman (see death notices from The Times 1984-88)

Adrian **Bloom** 1906-2005

After working in various horticultural nurseries, Adrian joined his father, Alan, a market gardener in 1926, and together they grew the family business into a wholesale nursery. Alan purchased Bressingham Hall, near Diss, in 1946, and with his other son Robert, they opened the Bressingham Steam Museum adjacent to the nursery. The 'Blooms of Bressingham' company was formed in 1985, with Adrian running the business after the death of his brother Robert in 1995. Adrian developed the world famous 6 acre garden known as 'Foggy Bottom' there. He travelled widely, and exhibited at the Chelsea Flower Show, where he was awarded the Royal Horticultural Society's Victoria Medal of Honour in 1972.

Adrian wrote about conifers and gardens; his books include

'Blooms best perennials and grasses'

'Gardening with conifers' 'Conifers for your garden'

'Year round garden' 'Conifers and heathers'

'Winter garden glory' and 'Summer garden glory'

Bressingham Steam and Gardens is now a popular tourist attraction with beautiful gardens to visit, working steam trains and a large garden centre.

1985 Margaret Thatcher was Prime Minister,' East Enders' the soap opera, starts, British Telecom start to phase out their red telephone boxes, Nissan's new car factory in Sunderland is built.

George Ewart **Evans** 1909-1988

Having lived at Blaxhall, Suffolk, where his wife was head teacher of the village school, George lived in Brooke from 1968.

Born in Abercynon, Rhonnda Cynon Taf in Wales, son of William and Janet. He is the youngest of 4 children on the 1911 census (there were eventually 11 children) his father a grocer, and the family living at Llanwonno, Glamorgan. He studied classics at Cardiff University and taught at Sawston Village College, Cambridgeshire before WW2. He married Florence in 1938 and was called up in 1941, serving in the RAF as a radio technician in 206 Squadron, Coastal Command. They lived with her mother in Enfield before moving to Blaxhall where he began to write stories, poetry, film and radio scripts for children, before pioneering the use of oral history, which he began in 1952. He interviewed many agricultural workers, some born in the 1890s, recording their everyday language and their rural trades, giving the reader a history of the transition from a manual to a mechanized working life during the twentieth century resulting in,

1956 'Ask the Fellows who cut the Hay', 1960 'The Horse in the Furrow'

1966 'The Pattern under the Plough' (in which he mentions a house in Bungay and George Borrow's use of words)

1969 'The Farm and the Village', 1970 'Where Beards Wag All'

1975 'The Days That We Have Seen', 1979 'Horse Power and Magic'

1983 'The Strength of the Hills', 1993 'The Crooked Scythe' and seven other books. Like Adrian Bell he witnessed the transition of agriculture employing many farm workers, with centuries' old skills, passed from generation to generation, where those traditions were being lost and forgotten. When Florence retired they moved to Brooke. He made many oral recordings in Bungay, about 7 miles from Brooke, became a founder member of the Oral History Society in 1969 and was influential in persuading many people to collect oral history. There are 254 items in the George Ewart Evans collection of recordings held at the British Library, covering many subjects from hares in Suffolk, to the last outbreak of bubonic plague near Ipswich, related by a local doctor, threshing using a flail, horse training, a thatcher's apprenticeship, driving a steam threshing engine, horsemen's secrets, shepherding, crow-keeping and much more.

Evans himself said "For more than a hundred years anthropologists have been going abroad to remote places to study the remains of bygone cultures: but here at home, and all around me, were the survivals of a rural culture that was at least as old as the early Middle Ages, but was being overwhelmed by the internal combustion engine."

Jonathan Mardle wrote about Evans in the EDP April 1969, and an appreciation of him was written by David Thomson which appeared in The Guardian in January 1988. David Gentleman, who has illustrated some of Ewart's books is his son-in-law.

The Museum of East Anglian Life, Stowmarket held an exhibition about Evans in 2016.

The Oral History Society grew from a day conference of the British Institute of Recorded Sound in 1969, when a committee was formed which established the Oral History Society in 1973.

Elizabeth **Smart** 1913-1986

Born in Ottowa, Canada, she later lived at The Dell, Flixton, near Bungay.

Best known for her book 'By Grand Central Station' 1945, Elizabeth had studied to become a professional musician in London, but gave that up to travel.

She is said to have fallen in love with the poet George Barker (1913-1991) who later lived at Bintry House, Itteringham on the Blickling Estate, Norfolk, through reading a volume of his poetry. She discovered that he was working at an academic post in Tokyo, paid for his flight to America where their affair began. She did not live with George Barker, who was married, but had four children by him.

She moved from London, after leaving her job with Harpers & Queens magazine, to the Dell at Flixton, later the home of John and Elsie Lidzey, the painter and potter. Elizabeth transformed the garden and converted this pair of former estate cottages into her home.

'A Bonus' collection of poems, 1977','The Assumption of rogues and rascals' 1978

'In the Meantime' 1984,   'On the side of the angels' 1994

She died on 4/3/1986 in London and was buried at St. Cross South Elmham churchyard, near the tomb of her daughter Rose, who had died in 1982.

EDP 7/3/86 Obituary by Ian Collins

'Elizabeth Smart who died aged 72 this week, was an accomplished writer and an adopted East Anglian. Born in Canada, she spent much of the last 20 years living happily at her cottage at Flixton near Bungay. She suffered a fatal heart attack while staying with a son in Soho, just when her work seemed destined for fresh acclaim.

Elizabeth Smart was known as the author of 'By Grand Central Station I sat down and wept'. This prose poem was described by critic Bridget Brophy as "one of the most shelled, skinned, nerve-exposed books ever written." The slim volume came from a devastating love affair she, the daughter of a wealthy lawyer, had with a hard-up and married poet. Neglected when first published in 1945 the book has belatedly reached a wide audience in recent years. Far from being the chronicler of a single cosmic love affair Elizabeth Smart was a born writer, mixing great sensitivity with hard headed practicality. Besides raising a family largely alone, and later caring for grandchildren, she worked in advertising and journalism. She was part of the post war Soho set of avant-garde artists. In Suffolk she wrote cookery books under pseudonyms; also creating a magical garden. In 1978 her 'The Assumption of Rogues and Rascals' was published, a loose sequel to Grand Central Station. There were additionally two volumes of poetry and frequent appearances at public readings. Shortly before her death she had been preparing for publication two texts drawn from her writings over several decades A prose and poetry selection 'In the Meantime' and 'Necessary Secrets: The Journals of Elizabeth Smart'

George Barker (1913-1991) was a contemporary of Dylan Thomas. Barker's 1950 novel 'The Dead Seagull' describes his affair with Elizabeth Smart. It was published five years after 'By Grand Central Station I Sat Down and Wept'.

Penelope **Fitzgerald** 1916-2000

Educated at Somerville College, Oxford, married to Desmond, a failing barrister, moved with their three children to Southwold in 1957. The children went to the local schools, their son going by bus to Sir John Leman high school in Beccles for a while. Penelope worked part time in The Sole Bay Bookshop and used her experience, along with her distinct memories of Southwold as a place " a very lonely town...sort of watery and marshy, with Constable skies", to write her second novel 'The Bookshop' published in 1978, but set between 1959 and 1960.

The family returned to London in 1961. It wasn't until she was in her sixties that Penelope was recognized as a writer, in 1979 her book 'Offshore' was shortlisted for the Booker prize and chosen by the judges—she was 63. She became famous for her book 'The Blue Flower', chosen in 1995 by twenty-five critics as their Book of the Year. In 1997 she was made an Honorary Fellow of Somerville college, and joined the Council of the Royal Society of Literature.

Mary **Wilson,** Baroness Wilson 1916-2018

Married in 1940 Sir Harold Wilson (he was Prime Minister 1964-1970 and 1974-1976), born at Diss, left here at 5 years old, the daughter of a Congregational Minister, Revd Daniel Baldwin, she spent her childhood in East Anglia. Her two volumes of poetry were published in the 1970s and sold very well.

There is a letter from Lady Mary dated 23/9/1977 from her London home to the treasurer of the church, when she loaned them her father's medal and photograph for an exhibition which started on 30th September, to celebrate the renovations of that church. "My father was minister at Diss (from 1913) until 1920 or 1921, and I was born there, but I remember little about it, as we left when I was young. The medal was presented to him for his work among the troops who were stationed or in transit near Diss during the first World War. I remember my uncle returning from the war driving a large Army lorry to our house in Frenze Road. I went to Diss a couple of years ago with Sir John Betjeman and saw the church before it was repainted, also the house where I was born."

A Mind's Journey to Diss

Dear Mary,

Yes, it will be bliss,

To go with you by train to Diss,

Your walking shoes upon your feet;

We'll meet, my sweet, at Liverpool Street.

That levellers may be reckoned

Perhaps we'd better travel second;

Or, lest reporters on us burst,

Perhaps we'd better travel first.

Above the chimney-pots we'll go

Through Stepney, Stratford-atte-Bow

And out to where the Essex marsh

Is filled with houses new and harsh

Till, Witham pass'd, the landscape yields

On left and right to widening fields,

Flint church-towers sparkling in the light,

Black beams and weather-boarding white,

Cricket-bat willows silvery green

And elmy hills with brooks between,

Maltings and saltings, stack and quay

And, somewhere near, the great North Sea;

Then further gentle undulations

With lonelier and less frequent stations,

Till in the dimmest place of all

The train slows down into a crawl

And stops in silence....Where is this?

Dear Mary Wilson, this is Diss.

<u>Reply to the Laureate</u>

Dear John,

Yes, it is perfect bliss

To go with you by train to Diss!

Beneath a soft East Anglian rain

We chug across the ripening plain
Where daisies stand among the hay;
We come to Diss on Market Day,
And cloth capped farmers sit around,
Their booted feet firm on the ground;
They talk of sheep, the price of corn;
We find the house where I was born—
   How small it seems! for memory
   Has played its usual trick on me.
The chapel where my father preached
Can now, alas, only be reached
By plunging through the traffic's roar;
   We go in by the Gothic door
   To meet, within the vestry dim,
   An old man who remembers him.
Now, as we stroll beside the Mere,
   Reporters suddenly appear;
   You draw a crowd of passers-by
   Whilst I gaze blandly at the sky;
An oak beamed refuge then we find,
The scones are good, the waitress kind;
   Old ladies, drinking cups of tea,
   Discuss their ailments cheerfully.
   Across the window-ledge we lean
   To look down on the busy scene,

And there, among the booths below,

Fat jolly babies kick and crow

As, wheeled by mothers young and fair,

They jolt around the Market Square.

School-children, dragging tired feet

Trail home along the winding street.

The church clock strikes a mellow chime

Just to remind us of the time;

We climb the hill as daylight fails,

The train comes panting up the rails,

And as the summer dusk comes down,

We travel slowly back to town.

What day could be more sweet than this,

Dear John, the day we came to Diss?

Diana **Athill** 1917-2019

Born in Norfolk, and educated at home until she was 14, she read English at Lady Margaret Hall, Oxford. Brought up in Hertfordshire and at Ditchingham Hall, near Bungay, where she recalls Sir Henry Rider Haggard reading the lesson in church. During WW2 she worked for the BBC Overseas Service and News Information Department and then joined the publishing firm Allan Wingate in 1948. In 1952 she became a founding director of that company which was renamed Andre Deutsch. Not retiring until the age of 75 she worked with many notable authors.

Diana started writing short stories in 1958, winning the Observer short story competition with 'The Return' in the same year.

'An unavoidable delay' collection of short stories published in USA in 1962.

'Don't look at me like that' 1967, 'Midsummer Night in the Workhouse' 2011, are her novels and she has written 10 autobiographical books, including

'Yesterday Morning: a very English childhood' 2002, 'Instead of a letter' 1963 'Stet' 2000, and 'Somewhere towards the end' 2008 which are assembled in 'Life Class'

She has appeared on 'Desert Island Discs, 2003, was awarded the OBE in 2009 and lived in London.

Philip **Wayre** 1921-2014

Co-founder, with his wife Jeanne, of the Otter Trust which opened at Earsham near Bungay, in 1978.

Philip was a well known TV presenter and author of wildlife books. He was educated at Sherborne School, and visited Norfolk for the first time in 1938. He served in the Royal Navy in the Second World War, reaching the rank of Lieutenant.

After the war he returned to Norfolk and worked for a farmer at Mileham near Dereham, buying his own farm in 1949, about which he said "I wasn't a successful farmer." He moved to Gt Witchingham and started rearing turkeys but turned his attention to his interest in wild animals.

Anglia Television was launched in 1959 where he was granted a five minute lunch time slot showing his animals. This led on to making programmes about natural history, including 'Twilight of the Tiger' filmed in India, with Terence Blacker as his assistant.

He opened Norfolk Wildlife Park in 1961, where he first tried to breed otters. His film 'The Vanishing Otter' did much to bring about awareness of the serious decline in otter numbers. After establishing the Earsham Otter Trust, where otters bred in captivity were released into the wild, he established four more otter reserves resulting in otter numbers increasing to about 12,000. He has been credited with saving the otter from extinction in England.

Philip was a member of the Norfolk Naturalists' Trust, the International Council for Bird Preservation, and the Flora and Fauna Preservation Society, and was appointed MBE in 1994.

His books include 'Pheasants: Including their care in the Aviary' 1961, 'A guide to the pheasants of the world' 1969, 'The River People' 1976, 'The private life of the otter' 1979 and 'Operation otter' 1989.

One of the Wayre's otters, Spade, had been hand reared by Jeanne and animal handler Pete Talbot. Spade played the starring role in the 1979 film 'Tarka the otter', based on Henry Williamson's novel.

Elizabeth Jane **Howard** 1923-2014

Born into a comfortably off family, with the same governess that had taught her mother and private teachers, she was educated at home. Her mother had been a dancer with the Ballets Russes. It is well known that she preferred her sons to her only daughter. Her father David, who had fought in WW1, was a director of the family-owned timber company.

Always called Jane, she joined a student repertory company in Devon in 1940, and met Peter Scott there when he was a Naval officer on sick leave. Their marriage in 1942 lasted for four years until they separated and they finally divorced in 1951.

Their daughter, Nicola, became the responsibility of Elizabeth's mother. Towards the end of her life she and Nicola became friends, and she left much of her estate to Nicola.

In 1950 Jane won the John Llewellyn Memorial Prize for her first novel 'The Beautiful Visit'. Living in London she had affairs with literary figures including Arthur Koestler, Laurie Lee and Cecil Day-Lewis. In her own words, she was 'a tart for affection most of my life.'

Her marriage to Jim Douglas-Henry, an Australian broadcaster, in 1958, was very brief. He incorrectly thought she had money.

She met Sir Kingsley Amis at the Cheltenham Literary Festival in 1962. After his divorce they married in 1965 and lived at 'Lemmons' a Georgian house in Barnet.

They separated in 1983, she referred to these years as 'my second fiddle period' during which her writing suffered. His book 'Lucky Jim' published in 1954, is a satire on life at one of the newer universities. In 1982 she wrote 'Getting it right', for which she also wrote the film script. In the 1990s she wrote the five-volume Cazalet series, about the ways in which English life changed during the war years in middle class society, especially for women. The final instalment 'All Change' was published in 2013. They have sold more than a million copies.

She and Louis de Bernieres met at the King's Lynn literary festival, and remained friends, with Louis visiting her at her home in Bungay more often as she became older and after he had moved to Denton in 2000.

She also wrote short stories, television plays, articles, film scripts and a book on food. She enjoyed cooking, tapestry work and embroidery.

Leaving London in 1990, she lived the latter part of her life at Bridge Street, Bungay, with many visitors to help her cope with her terror of loneliness. The artists who had lived near her in London moved to a property near her, where Chateaubriand had been 200 years previously. She became the Patron of Bungay Library. The waste land behind her house, which backs on to the river, was transformed by her into a nature reserve and she had a lake dug into an island in the river.

Arthritis troubled her and she died at her Bungay home, although her funeral service was in London. She was appointed CBE in 2000. Her autobiography 'Slipstream' was published in 2002.

Sir Malcolm **Bradbury** 1932-2000

Born in Sheffield, and after the family moved a couple of times, he attended West Bridgford grammar school in Nottingham, then studied English at University College, Leicester. Before becoming professor at the UEA's former school of English and American Studies 1970-74, he taught at the universities of Manchester, Indiana in USA, Hull and Birmingham. With Sir Angus Wilson he co-founded and later directed the MA course in Creative Writing at the UEA, in Norwich. This was the first university course of its kind in the country, which was attended by such writers as Ian McEwan and Kazuo Ishiguro, who was awarded the Nobel Prize in Literature in 2017.

He wrote novels, short stories, literary criticism and television plays and series.

'The History Man' 1975, was broadcast by the BBC as a four part serial in 1981, and is possibly his best known novel.

Awarded the CBE in 1991 for services to literature and knighted in the New Years Honours of 2000, he was a supporter of the British Council, serving as a foundation member of its literary advisory committee, bringing together writers and journalists, translators and academics from all over the world. He was a member of the Booker prize management committee, the British Association for American Studies, the Eastern Arts Association, the King's Lynn literary festival and the Norwich festival.

He felt that his teaching overtook his writing and that he had a couple more books he wanted to write.

He and his wife, Elizabeth, lived at Brockdish, (between Harleston and Diss) and later moved to Unthank Road, Norwich. They were known to be very hospitable. She converted novels and other writings into radio scripts for the BBC.

He died in Norwich and is buried in the churchyard of St Mary's church, Tasburgh.

Sir Arnold **Wesker** 1932-2016

Born in Stepney and raised in the east end of London, his mother, who had been born in Transylvania, was a cook, and his Ukranian father was a tailor's machinist; they both spoke Yiddish. Arnold began his schooling at a Jewish infants school, and spent the years of WW2 in London.

After a variety of labouring jobs he worked in the kitchen of the Bell Hotel, Timberhill, Norwich and served in the Royal Air Force for two years (1950-52) when he started an unpublished novel 'The Reed That Bent'.

He met his wife, Dusty, in Norwich, they married in 1958, and had three children. Her parents lived at Beck Farm, Redenhall near Harleston, where Wesker visited them, and also his sister, who lived with her husband at Hill House Farm, Wacton Common, near Long Stratton.

He has written 50 plays which have been translated into 18 languages and performed worldwide - he directed his own plays in Oslo, Rome, Munich, London, Stockholm and Havana as well as cities in the USA. Other works include essays, journalism, an autobiography, a children's book 'Fatlips' and poetry.

'Chicken Soup with Barley' 1958

'Roots' 1959 - commissioned by the Royal Court theatre in London, but rejected. Played at Coventry, following the success of 'Chicken Soup' there, and then to London after good reviews.

'I'm talking about Jerusalem' 1960

(The first presentation of the complete Wesker Trilogy was at the Royal Court Theatre in the summer of 1960; of these three plays Wesker says "My people are not caricatures. They are real (though fiction), and if they are portrayed as caricatures the point of all these plays will be lost. The picture I have drawn is a harsh one, yet my tone is not one of disgust - nor should it be in the presentation of the plays. I am at one with these people: it is only that I am annoyed, with them and myself.")

'The Kitchen' 1957, was made into a black and white film, starring James Bolam, in 1961

'As Much As I Dare' 1994- autobiography

He opposed nuclear weapons and played a leading role in the Committee of 100's demonstrations against the use of nuclear weapons.

He was awarded doctorates from the University of East Anglia, Queen Mary and Westfield College, London and Denison University in Ohio, and was knighted in 2006

All his papers, archived by Wesker himself, are held at the Harry Ransom Center at the University of Texas in Austin, USA.

Lindsay **Clarke** 1939

Lindsay was an only child, brought up by his caring parents in Halifax, where he attended Heath Grammar School. He studied English at King's College, Cambridge, and after a year in London took up the post of senior master for three years at a co-educational boarding school in Ghana. He was just 22, and Ghana had recently gained its independence (1957) from colonial rule. He used this experience in his first novel 'Sunday Whiteman', which was published in 1987 and shortlisted for the David Higham award. On his return to England Lindsay lectured in English at Gt Yarmouth College of Further Education, and then moved to Norwich City College as a co-ordinator of the Liberal Studies programme. He lived in Gissing, near Diss, from 1968 to 1970 when he moved to New Buckenham for a time, and later made a home in Aylsham, north of Norwich. From 1970 to 1978 he worked as a faculty member of Friends World College, an American Quaker foundation dedicated to cross-cultural experiential learning towards the ideals of World Citizenship and non-violent social change. The college had regional study centres in the USA, Mexico, Kenya, India and Japan, and as co-director of the European Centre, based in Norwich, Lindsay supervised students working on projects across Europe.

On moving to Somerset in 1985 he began his career as a freelance writer. His second novel 'The Chymical Wedding' won the 1989 Whitbread prize for fiction. The book is partly inspired by the life of Mary Anne Atwood who assisted her father to research the nature and history of alchemy, and its dual narratives cross time as people living in a small Norfolk village (much resembling Gissing) in the 1980s attempt to uncover the mystery of what had happened there in the previous century.

'Alice's Masque' was published in 1994 and 'Parzival and the Stone from Heaven' in 2001. Lindsay's life-long interest in myths, legends and the ancient world, are evident in his book 'Essential Celtic Mythology' and in his novels 'The War at Troy' (2004) and 'The Return from Troy'(2005), which were translated into many languages. His poetry has appeared in 'Stoker' 2006 and 'A Dance with Hermes' 2016.

Lindsay lectures in creative writing at Cardiff University and teaches writing workshops in Frome and London. He has had four radio plays broadcast on BBC Radio 4. His articles and reviews have been published in The London Magazine, England's oldest periodical dating from 1732, and Resurgence, a magazine which began in 1966 to cover environmental issues. He has recently written an article with Dr Julian Abel about the 'Compassionate Frome' project (a 'compassionate community' scheme tackling the connection between loneliness and ill health) which has featured in both Resurgence and The Guardian newspaper. (Feb.2018)

For many years Lindsay has worked as a creative consultant to The Pushkin Trust, which was founded in Northern Ireland by the Duchess of Abercorn. The core of its work is the Schools' Programme, which is a cross-community, cross-curricular, cross- border project encouraging all age school children from both sides of the sectarian divide and both sides of the border to write of their experiences and bring them together. On numerous visits to Ireland, Lindsay has worked on the project with teachers and senior civil servants, and in 2011 he co-ordinated a colloquium on A New Story for Ireland at St George's College, Windsor Castle.

Lindsay's latest novel 'The Water Theatre' was published in 2010 and was included in the Times's books of the year in 2011. The book was also long-listed for the Impac Dublin International Award. Following the death of his second wife, Phoebe Clare, who was a potter, he continues to live in Frome.

Richard **Mabey** 1941

Richard mentions aspects of his Berkhamsted childhood, playing outside in the deserted grounds of a large derelict mansion, bird watching, the changes in the seasons, in his books, such as 'Home Country' and 'Nature Cure'. His father worked for the Midland Bank, he had been working in Germany, but fearful of the coming war had returned to London in 1936 and moved to the home counties. As with most families, they used public transport as there was no family car. Richard, one of four children, attended Berkhamsted school as a day boy and excelled at chemistry and physics, which propelled him to St Catherine's College, Oxford, to start a degree in biochemistry. Within weeks he realized he wished to study PPE (politics, philosophy and economics), here he met Paul Foot, the journalist, attended lectures by Sir Isiah Berlin and became involved in the peace movement.

Richard became a lecturer in liberal studies at Dacorum College of further education, Hemel Hempstead. Two years later he worked as Senior Editor at Penguin Books, at a time when the company was expanding into the education market. He describes this as an enjoyable and experimental time, with much cooperation and creativity within the department, saying "My plan was to make the books more user-friendly by giving them the look of magazines, with integrated photographs, cartoons, news clips".

Highly aware of what was growing on his doorstep, in the hedges, fields and paths on his way to work, in woods he walked in, Richard built up an extensive knowledge of natural history. His first book 'Food for Free' was very successful and was published in 1972 at a time when people were thinking of self-sufficiency (John Seymour's book 'Self-Sufficiency' was published in 1976) .'The Unofficial Countryside' followed in 1976, this is a celebration of plants growing in the environment on the outskirts of London; David Cobham, who made the film 'Tarka, the otter', directed a film of Richard's book. TV documentaries followed, including working with John Craven on 'Countryfile' and 'In Deepest Britain' - the precursor to 'Spring-watch'. The film crew significantly shortened the time from filming to transmission, bringing immediate relevance to the viewer. Other TV documentaries include 'The Flowering of Britain' 1982 and 'White Rock, Black Water' 1986.

In 1980 Richard bought a 16-acre woodland, Hardings Wood, at Wittington in the Chilterns, vividly described in 'Home Country' including the 1987 October gale and his views of natural regeneration. He had established it as a successful community wood project which was used and enjoyed by the villagers, and by Richard 'as an immense private library of experiences and encounters'. Richard has written for the BBC Wildlife magazine since 1984 and for the Guardian, the Times, the New Statesman and other publications. In 1982 he became a member of the 'Nature Conservancy Council' (a government advisory body). He has been awarded honorary doctorates by St Andrews, Essex and East Anglia universities for his contributions to nature writing. His book, about the naturalist Gilbert White won him his first Leverhulme Fellowship in 1986, and the Whitbread Biography of the year.

Richard is a former director of the arts and conservation charity Common Ground and it became their aim to produce a book covering all plants indigenous to England, Scotland and Wales. The concept of 'Flora Britannica' led to the most comprehensive study, with contributions invited from the public as to local plant names and uses, locations and variations. Over 100,000 copies were sold, it won the National Book Award in 1996, and the President's Award of the Botanical Society. Richard won a Leverhulme Research Fellowship for this work.

The Chilterns had been Richard's home until 2002 when he moved to Norfolk - he had visited north Norfolk in his late teens and enjoyed holidays on the coast. He talks of his period of being unwell in 'Nature Cure' when he lived with friends and lodged in a friend's C16th house just a few miles from his current home in the Waveney Valley near Diss, which he moved to in 2004. In his book 'Weeds' he describes how surrounding farmland was known as the 'Hempland' and how the garden pond was used for 'retting' the hemp fibres. His good friend Roger Deakin lived nearby at Mellis Common - Richard wrote an obituary for Roger in 2006.

Since 1972 Richard has written more than thirty books, 'The Cabaret of Plants', 'A Brush with Nature', 'Beech-combings, the Narrative of Trees', his books explore our relationship with the world around us and cover the natural world, art, history, food, emotion, philosophy and a sense of humour. He is Patron of the John Clare Society (often including Clare's verse in his books), president of the Waveney & Blyth Arts, vice-president of the Open Spaces Society and was made a Fellow of the Royal Society of Literature in 2011.

Roger **Deakin** 1943-2006

Born in Watford, an only child, Roger was educated at The Haberdashers' Aske's Boys' School, then studied at Peterhouse, Cambridge under the auspices of Kingsley Amis. He worked as a copywriter while living in London and devised the National Coal Board slogan "Come home to a real fire". He married Jenny Hind in 1973, with whom he had a son Rufus, but the marriage was dissolved in 1982.

He taught French and English at Diss Grammar school from 1975 to 1978; the pupils gave him a leaving present of a goat, which was reported in the local press. In 1976 Oliver Bernard and Roger devised 'The Merry Tales of Skelton' which was performed on 14th October in Diss, with Roger reading Skelton's poetry.

In 1968 he had bought Walnut Tree Farm, in a semi-ruined state, situated on the edge of Mellis Common near Diss. This was an Elizabethan farmhouse which he rebuilt- the house and its surroundings were the subject of two BBC Radio 4 documentaries. Roger swam daily in the moat he had dredged, planted woodland, and harvested hay from his fields. In the words of Robert Macfarlane, "Roger was one of those rare people whose character and passion is to be found in everything he made, collected, drew or wrote..."

He contributed to and supported the newsletter 'Waveney Clarion' which ran from 1973 to 1984. It was started from the profits of the first Barsham Fair, near Beccles.

Roger kept copious notes of his meetings and activities, including the formation of the organization 'Friends of the Earth' from 1971. He talks of the first meeting in Paris with five countries attending in January, and that by December there were 1,000 registered supporters.

He was involved with FoE, writing notes 'In defence of or in celebration of nature and the countryside', and campaigns such as clean air 1994, road-building, saving whales; celebrities such as Michael Palin and Terry Jones were also involved in bringing these matters to the attention of the general public.

In the July 1979 copy of the Waveney Clarion Roger's article entitled 'Whales are disappearing' starts 'The Whale Declaration. It would be ironic if a society which seems to believe that big is beautiful were to consign the largest of the globe to extinction....Pity this busy monster, mankind.' In another letter Roger signs himself as Campaign Consultant. He was a friend of Andrew Lees (1949-1994), botanist and Campaign Director of FoE, who lived at Fleggburgh Common, Norfolk, although he died in Madagascar.

In Deakin's archive, housed at the UEA, there are many of his letters to the organization 'Greenpeace'.

The UK charity and lobby group Common Ground was founded in 1982 by Susan

Clifford and Angela King - their aim is 'to seek imaginative ways to engage people with their local environment...and have with the landscape that surrounds them.' Deakin was a founder member and director, and his 1983/4 'Holywells Park (Ipswich) conservation project' is in his archive. He felt there was a need to focus a new attitude to the countryside and its guardianship and promote the importance of common animals and plants, familiar places and our links with the past. He wanted Common Ground to promote practical links between nature and landscape, conservation and the arts. The organization was supported by John Fowles, and Richard Mabey was invited to write a preface/introduction to their proposed Parish Action Guide. Under the heading 'Why the need for Common Ground?' Deakin writes""Over recent years we have seen great changes in the character of our countryside. Hedge-rows have been grubbed up to make even bigger fields and ancient deciduous woodlands have been cleared for conifers or barley. Our countryside is losing its local character, distinctiveness and variety; familiar places and our links with the past are disappearing. The aim of Common Ground is to stimulate a new and imaginative approach to a problem that will become more urgent in the coming years - the widespread destruction of much that is wild and natural in Britain."

Deakin wrote articles for The Independent, such as 'Common Sense' April 2001, The Guardian and The Telegraph 'Crabwise through Cromer' June 2001, newspapers, as well as the BBC Wildlife magazine, including 'Brownsea Island'. He also made some TV documentary films including 'Stable-lads' in Newmarket.

He wrote poetry such as, 'Weasel Words', 'Waking Up', 'The Bold Navigator', 'Are such things possible?', and kept a folder of poems by Andy Bell (Clarion contributor), and others including his cousin Helen Kidd.

His book about wild swimming in the UK 'Waterlog' was published in 1999. Ken Warpole's (the Independent) review reads "To weave environmental and cultural concerns so deftly together in this enchanting and original travel book is a real achievement".

'Cigarette on the Waveney' 2005, Cigarette is the name of his canoe, is a BBC Radio 4 documentary about his canoe trip down the river Waveney.

'Wildwood' appeared posthumously in 2007, and covers a series of journeys to Kazakhstan, Kyrgystan, Lesbos and Australia that Deakin made to meet people whose lives are intimately connected to trees and wood.

Deakin died from brain tumour in August 2006, he received numerous letters and cards when he was ill. His notebooks, about his home and environs, written at his home of nearly 40 years were collected and edited as 'Notes from Walnut Tree Farm' by his friend Terence Blacker and Deakin's partner Alison Hastie, and published in 2008.

Winfried Georg Max **Sebald** 1944-2001

Born in Bavaria, one of three children, he was brought up by his grandfather in his early years in the village of Wertach, where they endured snow for five months of the year. His father who had joined the Army in 1929, reaching the rank of Captain, returned from a POW camp in 1947. Sebald, known as Max by his contemporaries, studied German literature at Friburg University and graduated in 1965. He was a lecturer at Manchester University 1966-69 and married Ute, from Austria, in 1967. From 1970 he was a lecturer at the UEA and became Professor of European Literature in 1987. In 1989 he became the founding director of the British Centre for Literary Translation; they hold an annual Sebald lecture, with contributions by Roger McGough, Michael Longley, A L Kennedy and more.

Sebald began writing fiction in his mid-40s; he always wrote in his native German.

Roger Deakin wrote of Sebald "I relish Max Sebald, as I love Thomas de Quincey, for his fearless digressions, for the sheer scope of his curious, cosmopolitan imagination and for his powers of free association. Why should I enjoy Sebald so much? because he is a great writer of landscape and memory: an archaeologist forever troweling his way through the larger of the stones, he always delves beneath every meadow and pasture."

Sebald's books often include his own photographs and other images:-

'Vertigo'1990, 'The Emigrants' 1992

'Rings of Saturn'1995 is an account of his walking tour of East Anglia, including Suffolk, both books translated from the German by the poet Michael Hulse and Adrian Bell's daughter Anthea Bell. "I felt like a journeyman in a century gone by, as out of place" says Sebald as he wanders through Suffolk. Deakin writes of the book "In the atmospheric mystery, its sudden horrors and swooning, altered states of consciousness, Sebald's work is almost Gothic."

'A place in the country'1998, 'On the natural history of destruction' 1999
'Austerlitz' 2001

Sebald was affected by the post war state of Germany and his finding out about the Holocaust, which was not mentioned as he was growing up. Eric Homberger (The Guardian) wrote "Silence and forgetting were conditions of his early life. Scorning the Holocaust industry and what he referred to as an official culture of mourning and remembering, Sebald disliked feel-good sentimental portrayals of terrible events, such as Thomas Keneally's 'Schindler's Ark'. He claimed no false intimacy with the dead."

He lived at Wymondham and Poringland. He died in a car crash near Norwich, and is buried at St. Andrew's churchyard, Framingham Earl.

Christopher **Reeve**   1946

The middle child of three brothers and one sister, Chris was born in Bungay where his parents had married in 1938 and his father worked at Clays, the printers. His mother, a teacher, had been governess to families in France and Holland. An avid reader, she loved poetry, learning many poems by heart, and it was hearing her recite them that inspired Chris with the same life long passion. Even at the age of 80 she committed the whole of the Rubaiyat of Omar Khayyam to memory.

Chris went to Bungay grammar school and during his teenage years started writing poetry, for two consecutive years winning the Lord Dunsany national poetry award. After a short career in book-selling, he attended St Andrews university, where he studied theology and art history, graduating with the degree of M. Theol. Hons. He worked as assistant museum curator at Moyses Hall Museum, Bury St Edmunds for five years before going to Italy for an extended period to develop an appreciation of Italian art, sculpture and architecture. With this experience he later studied as a part time mature student and graduated with the degree of B A Hons. in art history at the UEA.

On his return to Bury St. Edmunds he was appointed deputy curator of the Clock Museum, and subsequently Keeper of Fine & Decorative Arts, for St. Edmundsbury Borough Council based at the newly created Manor House Museum in 1990.

While living in Bury, he frequently returned home to visit his family, and eventually, following early retirement, moved back to Bungay in 2000 to care for his mother. He developed a keen interest in local history, and became the curator of Bungay Museum following the death of Dr Hugh Cane, who had founded it in 1963.

With his interest in local history it was a natural step to write about Bungay, his first book 'A Straunge and Terrible Wunder' investigating the story of 'Black Shuck', the phantom beast which caused mayhem and terror in the church during a terrible thunderstorm in 1577. He wrote a second book on the same subject 'Shock! The Black Dog of Bungay', in 2010, with David Waldron, and 'Paranormal Suffolk', exploring ghost stories throughout the region, in the previous year.

He has written 12 books in total, since 1988, including 'Bungay Through Time', 'The Waveney Valley - History, Landscape and People', 'Norwich – the Biography' 2011 and his most recent book 'Bungay at Work' 2017. He is currently writing a biography of Elizabeth Bonhote, the Georgian novelist. His books 'Secret Bungay' exploring mysterious and quirky aspects of the town, and a children's verse narrative 'The Dictionary Boy' were published in 2018.

Chris has published various booklets and articles on art topics, and continues to write poetry and narrative verse, often relating to local history, and performed for the Town Reeve's dinners, and on the stage of the Fisher Theatre.

He has contributed to the Oxford Dictionary of National Biography, with entries on Elizabeth Bonhote, John Childs and East Anglian artists. His research entailed visiting specialist libraries and archives throughout the country.

Immersed in the life and history of Bungay, Chris conducts guided tours, leads walks and gives lectures, is a member of the Town Trust, Waveney and Blyth Arts Group, the Bungay Society and remains curator of Bungay Museum.

_{Following the Butler Education Act of 1944, at the end of the war secondary education was provided by grammar schools for those children who had 'passed the 11+' and who showed an academic aptitude for future careers such as teachers, lawyers, doctors, civil servants, and 'secondary modern' schools for children who were expected to become shop assistants, builders, plumbers, hairdressers etc. The system was replaced in most counties by comprehensive schools during the 1960s and 1970s.}

Elaine Murphy 1947

Elaine and her first husband John Murphy bought 'The Grange' in Brockdish in 1976. She now lives here with her second husband, a scientist Michael Robb FRS.

Born in Nottingham, she attended grammar school in the city, as both her parents had done. Her father was deputy chief engineer at Boots (the chemist) – a large employer in Nottingham, where her mother had also worked. Elaine's two older brothers and their paternal grandmother made up the family.

Her grandmother slowly developed dementia, and there were often home visits from a female doctor, who impressed Elaine and increased her resolve to become a medical doctor. This meant changing schools at the age of 13-14 to study science subjects. Many years later she wrote to thank the two teachers who had given her so much encouragement and help at that time.

She studied medicine at the University of Manchester and married during her fourth year, but John was working in Wisconsin by then and it was a further two years before they set up home in London. After house jobs at Whipps Cross Hospital and further experience in geriatric medicine, Elaine studied psychiatry first in Birmingham, then at the National Hospital for Neurological Diseases, Queen Square and at the Royal Free Hospital and then St.Pancras, within the UCL family of hospitals. Professor Tom Arie had set up a specialist unit for the care of older people with mental disorders at Goodmayes Hospital in 1969, an innovative move which interested the Department of Health, and Elaine, and led her to working with older people and eventually becoming an academic at the University of London, researching depression in old age and running an NHS community service in south London. In 1983, at the age of just 37 she became the first female professor at the United Medical and Dental Schools of Guys and St Thomas' Hospitals and the first UK Chair in old age psychiatry.

This was a ground-breaking achievement in the early 1980s in England, and Elaine was much in demand for interviews on the subject of dementia on Woman's Hour and other BBC programmes, The Times newspaper, who profiled her career, and similar publications.

The government had set up an inquiry into the management of the NHS, headed by the CEO of Sainsbury's, who concluded that the NHS should be run by senior clinicians, especially doctors. Elaine was offered a management position in 'priority care' and at the same time became the vice chairman of the Mental Health Act Commission. She later became District General Manager for Lewisham and North Southwark Health Authority. Eventually, after retiring from the university she became Chairman of an NHS Trust and later a London Strategic Health Authority. Meanwhile she studied with Roy Porter the historian, at UCL for a PhD in medical social history, completing her PhD in 2000. She was encouraged by senior people in the NHS to apply for appointment to the House of Lords and two interviews and many months later Elaine was appointed Baroness Murphy of Aldgate in May 2004.

For 13 years, Elaine has participated actively in Mental Health, Health and Social legislation in the House of Lords, where she sits as a politically independent crossbencher. During 2018 she was involved with the mental health and mental capacity legislation although she is now taking a less active role in parliament than formerly.

Elaine has authored, co-authored or edited seven mental health related books, such as 'Dementia and mental illness in the old' 1986, and 'Dementia and mental illness in older people: a practical guide' 1993, ' After the Asylums' 1991 and 'The Falling Shadow' with Sir Louis Blom-Cooper QC and others, a report of the inquiry into the events leading up to a fatal incident at a mental health unit in Torbay in 1993. She has published about 250 papers on mental health topics and papers on the C17th and C18th social history, especially on 'Pauper Farms' including 'Mad farming in the metropolis, Part 1, A significant service industry in east London, and Part 2, the administration of the old poor law of insanity in the City and East London 1800-1834'.

Her 2015 book 'The Moated Grange' is the result of researching the history of her house and the people who lived there, in which she reflects on the history of south Norfolk over seven centuries. Her latest book 'Monks Hall - A Waveney Valley Manor', published 2018, is about an ancient house just over the county border in Syleham, which, like her own home, is located in the Waveney Valley.

(Interestingly Elaine has discovered a link between Monks Hall and Shelley Hall, both properties belonged to the Tilney family in the mid C16th.)

See also Terence Blacker p 92

Ian McLachlan 1947

Born in Scotland on 11th April 1947, just two years later the family moved to Ian's mother's hometown of Lowestoft. His father came from a family of seven brothers and two sisters; the grandparents ran a successful family grocery business. Ian's father Albert had wanted to be a journalist, but enlisted in the Army following a dispute with his father; he left home and ended up in the Royal Norfolk Regiment under the name McKenzie to avoid detection by his father. He met Ian's mother during the 1920s and, with the family situation resolved, he served as a McLachlan during WW2. During May 1941, on leave in Scotland, Ian's father saw Rudolf Hess fly over on his mysterious mission and later visited the Messerschmitt Bf 110 crash site at Eaglesham where a fellow soldier gave him some souvenir pieces.

Ian was educated in Lowestoft, and joined the Air Training Corps, but he was unable to join the RAF because of his poor eyesight. As a youngster he had an interest in aircraft which was inspired when his father handed on pieces of the Hess Messerschmitt. This was the catalyst for Ian's desire to learn more about the why and when of local aircraft crashes. Excavating the remains of a fallen Flying Fortress bomber and research into its loss saw his growing knowledge of the USAAF presence in East Anglia during WW2. Increasing involvement in aviation archaeology has led to him finding out about the aircraft, but above all about the pilots and crews, the human story, and ensuring that their names are remembered.

Aviation research archaeology was and is Ian's hobby, he worked at Pye Television Lowestoft from 1962-74; working for other companies he became a senior manager and travelled worldwide. He started writing about aviation, some of his seven books have become best sellers, such as '8th Air Force' and 'Final Flights', and are distributed in the USA and many English-speaking countries. He also writes articles for 'Flypast' and 'Aeroplane' magazines, and has taken part in many radio interviews. He is a lecturer with the WEA, and lives near Beccles.

Ian worked as a consultant to the Time Team 1998 programme 'Bombers', and is now involved in a successful TV series titled 'Plane Resurrection'. There will also be a 2-hour film made in conjunction with the American Commemorative Air Force to mark D-Day in 2019.

In his preface to 'Final Flights' Ian writes "In 1964, standing where 21 men died on a desolate marsh, I realised it was the men who counted…The least we can do is record the passing of these lives."

Ian's books :-

'Flights into History: Final Missions Retold by Research and Archaeology'

'Eighth Air Force Bomber Stories: Eye witness accounts from American Airmen and British Civilians in the Second World War'

'USAAF Fighter Stories: Dramatic accounts of US Fighter Pilots in Training and Combat over Europe in the Second World War '

'Night of the Intruders: First-hand Accounts of the tragic slaughter of USAAF Mission 311'

'Final Flights: Dramatic Wartime Incidents Revealed by Aviation Archaeology'

'Eighth Air Force Bomber Stories - A New Selection'

'USAAF Fighter Stories - A New Selection'

Terence **Blacker** 1948

Son of General Sir Cecil Hugh 'Monkey' Blacker, whose Army life took him to Aden, Germany and Northern Ireland, as well as postings within the UK.

Terence, born at Shelley Hall near Hadleigh in Suffolk, and his brother Philip, rode ponies from a very early age – their father's regiment was a cavalry regiment, their father an international show-jumper and their mother an accomplished horsewoman. The brothers were taught at home by a governess, Miss Curtis, who lived with them, until he was seven, when he was sent to Hawtreys boarding preparatory school, - this was his first experience of school. During every holiday Terence and Philip rode, taking part in competitive events, racing and show-jumping.

(After a successful career as a professional steeplechase jockey, Philip became a sculptor, particularly of horses. He created the life-size sculpture of Red-Rum which stands at Aintree Racecourse, and has completed many other sculptures of horses and people).

Terence went on to Wellington College in Berkshire and learnt to play the guitar there, which he still plays every day. He read English at Trinity College, Cambridge, there was little encouragement to write, but he worked on several stories. Continuing with his passion for horses, he drove almost daily to Royston at the crack of dawn to ride out with the 'first lot' (of racehorses) at 6.30am, breakfasting with the trainer, Willie Stephenson, and then riding out with the 'second lot' a couple of hours later, returning to Cambridge for his studies.

Following graduation Terence answered an advertisement in The Times for an assistant to Philip Wayre, who later established the Otter Trust at Earsham, to make a film about wildlife in India, a trip which took three months and about which Terence kept a diary, recording some of the surreal moments such as a tiger ambling along a track behind the elephant on which Terence was riding.

Terence abandoned horse racing, and went to live in Paris for 18 months, working in two bookshops, 'Shakespeare & Co' followed by 'Galignani', the oldest English language bookshop in Europe.

He came back to London in 1972, to work for the Hutchinson Publishing Group, starting as a salesman in Europe for two years, then became editor and finally editorial director of the paperback imprint Arrow Books. He lived in London in the 1970s and 80s and was married to Caroline Soper; they have two children. In 1978 they bought a house in Wortham, near Diss, from Moray Rash, the son of the writer Doreen Wallace.

During this time, under the pseudonym of Jonty Lejeune, Terence wrote a satirical column for the book trade's magazine 'Publishing News', which he found a very liberating experience, and he began writing comedy books. He edited a very successful book based on the sitcom 'The Young Ones', and completed his first novel 'Fixx', published in 1989, to critical acclaim. He has written a whole series of children's books under the umbrella title of 'Ms Wiz', as well as 'Boy2Girl' and 'The Transfer'.

Terence became a full-time writer in 1983 and in 1990 was approached by 'The Sunday Times' to write a weekly column under the name of Harvey Porlock. He wrote a regular opinion column, under his own name, once or twice a week for 'The Independent' from 1998 to 2015.

Set in the imaginary village of Burthorpe, near to Diss, his third novel 'Revenance' 1996, is a ghost story which resurrects the memory of John Skelton, the poet, and includes the appearance of a mediaeval woman Margaret Cowper. His other novels 'The Fame Hotel' and 'Kill Your Darlings' were published in 1992 and 2000. In 1994 he was a writing fellow at the UEA creative writing course led by Malcolm Bradbury and Rose Tremain.

Terence wrote three books with his friend and author of 'The Henry Root Letters' Willie Donaldson. Willie died in 2005, and a few months later Terence wrote his biography, as he puts it 'under the catchy title' of 'You Cannot Live as I Have Lived and Not End Up Like This: The Thoroughly Disgraceful Life and Times of Willie Donaldson'.

In 2001, Terence moved to Rushall with Angela Sykes, now director of the Corn Hall in Diss. Over the past ten years, he has been writing and performing his own songs on the guitar and ukulele. He has released three CDs of his songs; 'Lovely Little Games' in 2012, and 'Sometimes Your Face Don't Fit' in 2016, and 'Enough About Me' in 2018. In 2013 he took his show 'My Village and Other Aliens' based on his songs and stories to the Edinburgh Fringe. He regularly appears at festivals, theatres and folk clubs, performing and singing his songs.

Roger Deakin was a very good friend of Terence until his death in 2006. Roger left unpublished notebooks about his home and environs, which, with Roger's partner Alison Hastie, Terence collected and edited as 'Notes from Walnut Tree Farm'.

Terence's fifth novel 'The Twyning' came out in 2013; this is a story of a rat kingdom underground 'at war' with a Victorian city above them.

In the same year 'Yours E.R: A Regal Correspondence' which imagines the letters of Her Majesty the Queen written to a former private secretary between the London Olympics (of 2012) and the birth of Prince George (born 2013), was published.

'Racing Manhattan' a novel for young readers was published in 2016.

In 2017 Terence was elected a Fellow of the Royal Society of Literature.

Ian **Carstairs** 1948

Ian was born in Perth; with the arrival of a younger brother the family moved to London, where their father worked in computer technology and insurance. Following grammar school Ian trained as a graphic designer and photographer at Epsom School of Art in Surrey, where his interest and love for the natural world was fostered.

He worked for a while for a publisher in York and then became assistant Director of the Moors Centre in the Esk Valley. Later he and his wife, Jan, bought a derelict house with an acre of garden in the Vale of Pickering which they restored, Ian became self-employed and regularly gave talks about major wildlife and countryside projects, with which he had become involved.

He has undertaken many voluntary roles in connection with conservation – he was a Secretary of State's Appointed Member to the Board of the North York Moors National Park Authority, where he became Deputy Chairman. He was approached by the Heritage Lottery Fund and served on the England Committee for two years and was then Chairman for four years of the Yorkshire and Humber Committee of the HLF when its operations were regionalised.

The River Derwent Campaign for the River Derwent Group was co-ordinated by Ian (a ten-year House of Lords Test Case which legally defined the meaning of a River for the first time in history) and he acted as 'honest broker' to negotiate a solution to the Review of the Selby Coalfield Planning Consent, under EU Habitats Directive Regulation

Ian set up the Carstairs Countryside Trust - a charity - in 1989, which has brought numerous sites of great natural, archaeological and historical importance in Yorkshire into protective ownership for the benefit of future generations and diversity of wildlife, and only stood down from this role three years ago. Ian was made an MBE for services to conservation in 1995 and an OBE for services to Heritage in 2007.

He has been a member of the National Rivers Authority and the Forestry Commission's Regional Advisory Committees. The National Federation of Anglers and he received the Golden Scale and the Mark of the Golden Scale Club for his work on the Yorkshire river Derwent.

Although Ian states "I've never really considered myself a writer, more that I have produced things in pursuit of the wider purpose of a cause", his books, which include hundreds of his own photographs, are about landscape and conservation, much of the work spearheaded by Ian, and convey his passion to protect the quality of the countryside and built environment:-

'2nd Official Guide Book to the North York Moors National Park'

'The Yorkshire River Derwent Moments in Time '– charts a complex series of community action and details about the river.

'A Harvest of Colour- Saving Cornfield Flowers in North East Yorkshire'– a unique project spearheaded as an exemplar of how individuals can achieve an amazing rescue of seriously threatened plants.

'The Marsh of Time Saving Sutton Common' – another complex project to secure and save an internationally significant Iron Age site (with others)

'Moods of the North York Moors' – a photo book

'A Portrait of York '– a photo book

'A Portrait of Hull' – a photo book

'Moods of the Yorkshire Coast' – a photo book

'A Portrait of the Waveney Valley' – a photo book

With Ian's wife having family connections in the town they moved from Yorkshire to Harleston where he is involved in community activities such as raising awareness of the Swifts which visit every year, flags above shop fronts which make the town look welcoming and inform residents of events such as a food and drink festival in the town, free car parking, the cranes peace initiative and road traffic and safety.

Here in south Norfolk Ian enjoys the big skies, especially the night sky, and continues to be involved in planning issues and campaigns and educates against increasing light pollution. He retains some roles in Yorkshire; he is Vice-Chairman of York City Charities (Fothergil Homes sheltered housing), trustee responsible for financial and strategic development, and is president of the North Yorkshire Moors Association.

Ian's main concern for the immediate future centres on the growing financial pressures for voluntary and conservation organisations, and the potential physical effects on the countryside of post-Brexit Britain, stemming from the loss of EU funding and regulation. He believes, sadly, that there is a massive challenge for all who care about the interconnectedness of its natural, historical, archaeological, palaeo-environmental features, to ensure that they are not diminished in an era where the rule books are being torn up and funding is disappearing.

Basil **Abbott** 1950

Basil was born in Diss, and read English at the UEA from 1974, where he won the Charles Herbert-Smith Memorial Prize for English Literature. He wrote an M Phil thesis on the Old English poem Beowulf. Whilst a student at UEA he attended Malcolm Bradbury's Creative Writing Seminars.

Basil writes "I have been contributing to the press all my adult life, with articles and reviews and am East Anglian correspondent for Plays International magazine. Short stories of mine have appeared in The Guardian; in Angus Wilson ed. 'Writers of East Anglia' (Secker & Warburg 1977); Maggie Gee ed. 'For Life on Earth' (UEA, 1982); Suzi Blair ed. 'Paper Clips' (New Fiction 1999) etc.

I have published my own books of stories and articles. As Diss Museum Manager I have written scripts for local pageants and festival events, including CDs and films about historical figures such as John Skelton, John Betjeman and Thomas Paine.

In 2017, at the Liverpool Irish Festival, I gave a presentation called The Flush Hall Murder, which I researched and wrote. The CD was distributed on 30,000 copies of True Crime magazine.

I was also editor of the Diss Town Guide for over 30 years.

The projects I have co-ordinated have won several awards, including a Museums & Heritage Award for Excellence. 2019 will see the centenary of the R34 airship's double crossing of the Atlantic and return to Pulham. For this I have adapted the Log of the R34 as a radio script, and written scripts to be performed at various events."

Charles **Christian** 1950

Charles was brought up in an old house in Scarborough, his father had served in the RAF in Borneo, his mother enjoyed literature and was the founder member of the local writers' circle. They ran a 'fancy goods' shop on the sea front, very busy in the summer, very quiet in the winter months.

At 11 Charles went to Scarborough Boys' High School and then on to Leeds University where he studied politics. While at school in the 6th form, he had his first story accepted by Argosy magazine, and also wrote articles for the local newspaper. Along with a photographer friend he wrote a series about the different areas of Leeds, comparing and contrasting the wealthy and the poverty-stricken regions of the city. From Leeds he moved to London for another period of studying, this time at law school and he became a barrister.

Writing at a time when technology was advancing rapidly, it was a natural step to combine the law and technology, especially as privacy laws did not exist in the embryonic electronic communications era. In 1995 Charles won the National Newspapers Technology journalist of the year prize. He had already worked in PR at the launch of the earliest micro-computers and written on technology and the law for the insurance press as well as a weekly column for a medical magazine.

For 20 years Charles published his own newsletter 'The Legal Information Technology Insider', and wrote for trade and technical publications, including during 1999, 'How to deal with the Millennium Bug'. There has been a technological communications revolution between the mid-1980s and now, and many concerns were expressed towards the end of 1999 as to whether computers would survive the millennium date change – of course they did!   During this time Charles had some short science fiction stories published, and has since written

'This is the Quickest Way Down' 2011, 'Secret Cargo' 2013,

'Tomorrow's Ghosts'2014, 'Writing Genre Fiction- Creating Imaginary Worlds: The 12 Rules' also 2014, which has sold 10,000+ copies,

'A travel Guide to Yorkshire's Weird Wolds: The Mysterious Wold Newton Triangle' 2015

When asked what draws Charles to write about urban myths, the weird and folklore, he cites his childhood home, early memories of Sledmere House, just 20 miles from Scarborough and its eccentric owners plus ghost hunting expeditions whilst at university.

He now writes a weekly podcast 'The Weird Tales Radio Show' which covers urban myths and ghost stories from around the world, this has a huge following in the USA. He has started work on writing 'Saints and Sinners' about Saxon saints and kings and queens, and a second book about the legends and folklore of the Waveney Valley.

He lives near Bungay, having moved to Norfolk from London over 15 years ago.

Louis **de Bernieres** 1954

Louis moved to Denton, near Bungay, "in time to join the Millennium celebrations." He and his two sisters were brought up in Surrey. His Army officer father was pleased that Louis was awarded an Army scholarship at the age of 15, whilst he was at Bradfield public school in Berkshire.

This led to Sandhurst; four months of training there highlighted Louis' lack of interest in the academic side of military life and his total unwillingness to conform to a rigid structure. Louis had no knowledge that his father had to repay the school fees and a discharge fee, until his father told him when he was 40 years old. Louis promptly paid them back, having asked the bank to calculate the current value of the expense, and his parents went on a cruise!

After Sandhurst he worked as a landscape gardener for several months, before traveling to Columbia to work on a hacienda as a tutor to four children for a year.

He studied Philosophy at Manchester University, continuing with the gardening part time, and went on to teach Philosophy to adult education classes in London, while living in Brixton. There was a period of working in a Stoke Newington garage - Louis was the only one there who knew how a Morris Minor engine works - between his time at Manchester and Leicester teacher training college. Friendship brought Louis to East Anglia, and he taught English and Drama at Ipswich for three years. Louis describes one of the most interesting periods of his life after achieving a distinction with his MA at the London Institute of Education, as when he was a supply teacher for the ILEA at Wandsworth. When the ILEA was abandoned, there was no job, but Wandsworth took him back to work with school truants for three years. During this time Louis wrote his Latin American Trilogy, 'The War of Don Emmanuel's Nether Parts', 'Senor Vivo and the Coca Lord', and ' The Troublesome Offspring of Cardinal Guzman'.

Louis is an enthusiastic musician and plays the flute, guitar and mandolin, as well as building musical instruments himself. Music occurs in all his books, not least 'Captain Corelli's Mandolin', for which he won the Commonwealth Writers' Prize. The book, resulting from a holiday in Cephalonia, was turned into a film in 2001. He researched the material for 'Birds without wings' in Turkey by regular visits to the Turkish archives where he was helped by the ambassadorial staff, who have remained his friends. Louis regards this as his best book, which has sold over half a million copies; it was short-listed for the 2004 Whitbread Novel Award and the 2005 Commonwealth Writers' Prize.

Louis has travelled widely including to Australia, from where he found his material for 'Red Dog', Canada where his grandfather lived and where he met his grandfather's friends, spending three months teaching creative writing at Calgary University, and undertaking two North American book tours.

He is now writing a trilogy, the first book 'The Dust That Falls From Dreams' was published in 2015 , the second part 'So Much Life Left Over' in 2018.

A book of short stories, 'Labels and other Stories' will be published in 2019. He is currently recording all the songs he has ever written, 'With the Bookshop Band' appeared in 2018, with at least three more CDs to follow.

Louis also writes poetry and has three books published ,'Imagining Alexandria', 'Of Love and Desire', and 'The Cat in the Treble Clef' 2018.

David **Merrifield** 1957

At the age of 15, David moved with his parents from Goodmayes in Essex; he was born in St Marylebone, London; to Ormesby St Margaret, attending school in Gorleston. He worked for HM Customs & Excise for 40 years, and now lives in Lowestoft, with his second wife. He writes poetry, short stories and plays as well as novels.

His books include 'The Farmer' 2011, 'The Tree Doctor' 2013, 'We Need a Revolution' 2013, 'I've got your number' 2016, and 'The Somerby Tree' 2017.

Julie **Myerson** 1960 born in Nottingham .

Her fourth novel 'Something Might Happen', 2003, was long-listed for the Man Booker Prize for Fiction. The narrative explores the devastating effect of a brutal murder on the inhabitants of a small seaside town in Suffolk (Southwold?)

Esther **Freud** 1963 born in London

the daughter of Lucian Freud, the painter, and Bernadine Coverley, at the age of 16 she trained as an actress in London. She has worked in both television and the theatre, lives in London and has a home in Walberswick near Southwold.

Her novels include 'Hideous Kinky' 1992, which was made into a film starring Kate Winslet, 'The Sea House', 'Peerless Flats', 'Summer at Gaglow', 'The Wild', 'Lucky Break', 'Love Falls' and 'Mr Mac and me'- set in 1914 in a Suffolk coastal village, (Walberswick) 14 year old Thomas Maggs is intrigued by the visitor Charles Rennie Mackintosh and his wife. Esther also writes travel and other articles for newspapers and magazines, and teaches creative writing.

Tom **Cox** 1975

Born in Nottingham, at the age of 13 he became obsessed with golf, practicing and playing to achieve a handicap of two by the time he was 18. His interest in music and writing drove him to write his own publication about music and he was then employed by the New Musical Express until 1997. He came to the attention of music press editors, Radio One disc jockeys and from 1997 to 2000, he wrote about pop music for The Guardian, becoming the paper's Rock Critic in 1999. He has also written articles for The Sunday Times, The Times, The Observer, The Mail On Sunday, and other newspapers.

His memoir of his time as a teenage golf rebel 'Nice Jumper' was published in 2002, which was shortlisted for the National Sporting Club/Ladbrokes' Best Newcomer award. His other book about golf is 'Bring me the Head of Sergio Garcia' 2007 which was listed for the William Hill Sports Book of the Year award.

Tom lived in Norfolk for 13 years, on the outskirts of Diss, where he wrote a lot about Norfolk in his 'cat' books. His cat book 'The Good, The Bad and the Furry' 2013 was included in the Sunday Times bestseller list. He covers many genres, nature, humour, fiction, folklore, music and golf, and left journalism altogether in 2015 to write regular pieces about the countryside and his interests for his voluntary subscription website. He has included Norfolk in his book '21st Century Yokel' 2017, written from his Devon home; this book was crowd funded in a record breaking seven hours. Crowd funding is a method of funding a project or venture by raising small amounts of money from a large number of people, typically via the internet.

Luke **Wrigh**t 1982

Brought up in Essex, Luke attended Colchester sixth form college. He began writing and performing poetry when he was 17 as well as writing songs for the band Koonunga, where he enjoyed performing. The band separated at the end of 1998, by which time Luke had seen John Cooper Clarke perform at Colchester Arts Centre. He was also influenced by Ross Sutherland, poet, who gave Luke help and support and together they formed the Aisle 16 live poets collective which was the Time Out Critics' Choice of the Year list for its theatre show 'Poetry Boyband' in 2005. In 2006 he began creating solo shows of his poetry. In the same year he ran the Poetry Arena at the annual Latitude Festival held at Henham park near Southwold, which he continues to do. He has won two national awards for his verse narrative and has performed at the Edinburgh Festival. In 2009 Luke established Nasty Little Press, an independent publishing house focusing on poets better known for their live performance work. He lives in Bungay and is a supporter of Bungay library and the Fisher theatre. He has written 'What I learned from Johnny Bevan' 2016, 'The Toll' 2017,and 'Frankie Vah' 2018, his second verse play.

He has appeared on television on several occasions, on BBC Look East for National Poetry Day 2016, and on BBC Radio 4,3 and 5, 'Oh England Heal My Hackneyed Heart' on The Verb, Radio 3, 2017

Sandra D**elf**,

author of 'Keep Smiling Through' writes

"My father, a Lowestoft man, was a Prisoner of War during WW2. I had always known there were a large number of letters from him kept in an old fashioned attaché case in my mother's house. From time to time she would sit and read one. He died, quite young, in 1962. When my mother died they were one of the first things I looked for and made sure survived.

Eventually I got round to looking at them. There were 176. Once I put them into date order I found there were stories running through the letters, and they contained a lot of information about how they ran their everyday lives inside the camps. This included their football leagues and the importance of Red Cross Parcels and the sharing out of the contents. This inspired me to write and publish the book.

I have always been interested in history, it was my favourite subject at school, and I volunteer at Lowestoft Museum. I also belong to a local family history group and a local writing group.

I am now a multi-genre author having recently also penned and published a fiction book for very young children. 'Marcie and the Lonely Daisy' is about friendship between different kinds of people. It has illustrations by Kirsty Hawkes."

Local Newspapers

1873-1877 The Lowestoft Weekly Journal and Yarmouth and County Record

1877-1902 The Lowestoft Journal and Yarmouth and County Record

1902-1917 The Lowestoft Journal and Suffolk County Record, Lowestoft Weekly Standard 1906, Today's Lowestoft Journal is published by Archant

Waveney Valley Weekly News ran from April to September 1872

Harleston Advertiser ran from September 1853-April 1854

Diss Express, founded in November 1864 as the Diss Express and Norfolk & Suffolk Journal, The Diss Mercury, weekly from 1994

South Norfolk News from 1953-55

Harleston and Diss Express, Beccles and Bungay Journal

There are many pamphlets and small books relating to local history, buildings and people to be found in libraries in the Waveney Valley market towns.

Academics, living in the area, have written books on their specialist subjects, such as John Mitchell, the art historian, and many others.

Local artist Sir Alfred Munnings, born at Mendham, wrote his autobiography in 3 volumes between 1950 and 1952, 'An Artist's life' 'The Second Burst' 'The Finish'

Other local people

Samuel Wilton Rix

Born 1806 in Diss, married Eliza 1833, having moved to Beccles in 1831 to work as a solicitor.

He was interested in history, and collected much material about the history of Beccles, newspaper cuttings, legal documents and catalogues. He became a Town Councillor in 1836, and was Mayor from 1863-1865. Much of the material is archived with Suffolk Record Office.

He talks of "travelling outside the 'Star' coach on 23rd March 1831, through blinding dust and cold rain. A ninepenny letter was my precursor, penny postage and electric telegrams being then unknown. The 'Yarmouth Star' passed through Beccles, on its upward journey, every morning at a quarter past six, giving notice of its approach by a clanging horn and the thunder of heavy wheels upon the pavement."

Clementia Taylor (nee Doughty) 1810-1908

Born in Brockdish (lived at The Grange), she became the governess to the daughters of a local Unitarian minister who ran a boys' boarding school in Hove. She married in 1842 Peter Taylor, a cousin of her pupil's; he was partner in the family firm of Courtaulds and later became a Liberal MP for Leicester. From their home Aubrey House, Notting Hill, London, she became involved with the anti-slavery movement, in the campaign for Italian unification, improving education and she chaired the very first meeting of the Committee of the London National Society for Women's Suffrage in 1867. She died in Brighton in 1908.

Lillie Marion Springall 1898-1969

She lived at Thurston, near Bury St Edmunds, and wrote 'Labouring life in Norfolk villages 1834-1914' published in 1936 by George Allen & Unwin.

Mentioned by Lilias R Haggard in 'Norfolk Life' Lilias states "it covers politics, work and wages, social conditions and includes some interesting letters from emigrants and details of family budgets."

Sir John Mills 1908-2005

Born in Felixtowe he went to the Sir John Leman School, and lived in New Market, near Beccles Church. Actor and director for the both the film industry and television, he was knighted in 1977 and has published two autobiographies, 'Up in the Clouds, Gentlemen Please' and 'Still Memories'.

James Arthur Read 1878

Brought up at Frestons Farm, Mendham, child-hood friend of Alfred Munnings, who lived nearby, he became a journalist in New York, and wrote of his home in great detail in 'North Sea Scud and Florida Sun'.

Dorothy Mary Hodgkin (nee Crowfoot)

Born 1910 in Egypt, educated at Sir John Leman School, Beccles, Somerville College, Oxford and PhD in Cambridge. She worked in x-ray diffraction of crystals of the digestive system, studied the structure of penicillin, and the B12 vitamin and of insulin. She was made a Fellow of the Royal Society in 1943 and was awarded the Nobel Prize for chemistry in 1964.

Charles Julian Tennyson

Born 1915, great grandson of Alfred Tennyson. He wrote 'Suffolk Scene', in which he writes about the river Waveney, and 'Rough Shooting'. He served as Captain in the British Army, was killed in March 1945 and buried at Taukkyan War Cemetery, Myanmar.

David Woodward

Born in Beccles in 1930 and educated at Sir John Leman School. He served for two years in the Fleet Air Arm (National Service) and went on to study at Writtle Agricultural College. His books include 'A Garland of Waveney Valley Tales', 'Larn Yourself Silly Suffolk', 'Tatterlegs for Tea', and 'Beccles Schooldays 1930-1948'. He lived in Frostenden, Suffolk.

Kate Chennour

Lived in Harleston for a while where she researched and wrote 'The Victorian Common. A study of Harleston Common and its inhabitants during the Victorian Period' 2017

River Waveney Trust

In 2013 the trust produced a 34 page booklet 'Discover the River Waveney From Source to Sea', foreword by Richard Mabey, text by Geoff Doggett and Andrew Mackney and some photographs by Ian Carstairs.

World War 2

During WW2, from 1943 to 1945, the United States Air Force (USAF) occupied several air fields in this area.

The 93rd Bomb Group (BG) at Hardwick

the 100th BG at Thorpe Abbotts

the 446th BG at Bungay

the 448th BG at Seething

the 491st BG at Metfield

Memoirs and diaries, letters home and flight logs from this time can be seen at local museums. An extract from the memoir of Albert B. Sanders perhaps summarizes their experiences "I see that nowhere in these wanderings have the English people or especially the English pilots been given the kind of credit they deserve. We colonists were probably always treated with more courtesy and respect than we deserved for to a great extent we were ugly Americans. We were paid about four times the amount that the equivalent English rank was and far too many English girls thought that we were all rich. The English were brave in the face of death and patient in the long food lines and severe rationing. And in addition to their pilots winning the Battle of Britain, thus saving mankind from Hitler's eventual control, they continued to fly night bombing missions in spite of heavy losses due to flak and the deadly radar equipped German night fighters."

Museums

93rd BG, Hardwick, near Topcroft, south Norfolk

100th BG, Thorpe Abbotts, near Diss

446th BG, Norfolk & Suffolk Aviation Museum, Flixton, near Bungay

448th BG, Seething Control Tower Museum, near Bungay

491st BG, Metfield, area now returned to agricultural use.

More information at the 2nd Air Division Memorial Library, Norwich Forum,

Tech-Sgt John Appleby, an American airman stationed here, and who visited Beccles church, wrote 'Suffolk Summer', when in 1945 he recorded his friendships with Suffolk people and his explorations of the unspoilt Suffolk countryside.

Publications

Waveney Life magazine 1991-?, monthly magazine published by Vic Mayes, Beccles

Waveney Clarion

The first Barsham Fair was held at Beccles in 1972, bringing together 'alternative society' people who had left city life in search of a simpler life-style and personal freedom. At a time of no mobile phones or internet, a good way to keep in touch was by a monthly newspaper. The 'Clarion' was launched in 1973 with a grant of £100, and covered many wide-ranging subjects from rural housing, energy issues, organic agriculture to local schools and local music. The Barsham Fair became an annual event, the Clarion was supported by a wide group of writers, advertisers, designers, readers, musicians and distributors. The publication ceased at the same time as the Barsham Fair in 1984. From the Clarion

> In 1970 few people would have considered commuting from Norfolk or Suffolk to work in London, but with cheaper homes, some for renovation, available, East Anglia became attractive to people looking for an 'alternative life-style'. They were searching for self-sufficiency, personal freedom, self-reliance, greater artistic and musical license and the chance to live away from the city.

> The new-comers met other like-minded people and in 1971 formed the East Anglia Arts Trust; their first event, Barsham Fair, was held at Roos Hall, Beccles in 1972. This was very successful, and with some of the profits from the fair, it was decided to create a monthly newspaper. At a time before mobile phones and the internet, this was a way of connecting with readers to cover a wide range of topics which included future fairs, rural housing, energy issues, alternative theatre, local history, local schools, growing your own food, organic agriculture, the local music scene, local walks, real ale, the promotion of cycling and more; the publication was led by Sandra Bell.

> 'The Clarion' was usually steered by an inner group of 6-10 people, and was supported by a wide range of writers, advertisers, designers, distributors, musicians and readers. It was featured in the 'Sunday Times' colour magazine, and ran from 1973 to 1984.

> Roger Deakin was a contributor and supporter.

Index

Abbott B.	Page 96	Childs J.	27
Adair A. Maj Gen Sir	63	Christian C.	96
Alderson E. Brig Gen Sir	56	Clarke L.	82
Amyot T.	25	Cobbett W.	13
Amyot T. Dr	26	Cobbold R.	31
Athill D.	77	Collins W.	46
Baker S. Sir	40	Conrad J.	56
Barbauld A.	17	Cox T.	99
Barber M.	60	Crabbe G.	20
Bartholomew A.	37	de Berneries L.	97
Bell A.	66	Deakin R.	85
Betjeman J. Sir	70	Defoe D.	11
Blacker T.	92	Delf S.	100
Blomfield E.	27	Evans G.	71
Blomefield F.	13	Everitt H.	59
Bloom A.	70	Fitzgerald E.	45
Blyth J.	59	Fitzgerald P.	73
Bonhote E.	19	Freud E.	99
Borrow G.	37	Galpin F.	59
Bradbury M. Sir	80	Gillingwater E.	13
Bransby J.	23	Gowing J.	19
Broome W. Dr	9	Haggard R.H. Sir	46
Candler C.	58	Haggard L.	61
Carstairs I.	94	Hardy T.	45
Chateaubriand F.	23	Howard E.J.	79
		Mabey R.	83

106

Maggs J.	35	Wayre P.	78
Mann E.	57	Wesker A. Sir	81
Manning T.	25	Williamson H.	62
McLachlan I.	91	Wilson M. Baroness	74
Merrifield D.	99	Woodforde J.	15
Murphy E.	89	Woolf V.	60
Myerson J.	99	Wordsworth W.	24
Orwell G.	68	Wright L.	100
Paine T.	14	Wright W.A.	45
Ransome A.	60	World War II	102
Reeve C.	88		
Scott J.B.	28	Any errors or omissions are unintentional	
Sebald W.G.	87		
Sewell A.	39		
Skelton J.	4		
Smart E.	72		
Strickland A.	29	NRO Norfolk Record Office	
Suckling J. Sir	7	RGS Royal Geographical Society	
Trollope A.	40	FoE Friends of the Earth	
Ulph E.	66	UEA University of East Anglia	
Wallace D.	63	HLF Heritage Lottery Fund	

Published by Walton Associates
Alburgh, IP20 0BS